Working Deerhounds
Lurchers and Longdogs

The author's Gwen

Working Deerhounds Lurchers and Longdogs

Bill Doherty

Goldfinch Publications
2006

First published in England in 2006 by
Goldfinch Publications
19 Park Road, Ashington, Northumberland, NE63 8DZ

Printed in Wales by Gwasg Gomer, Llandysul

ISBN   0-9551973-1-7
ISBN 978-0-9551973-1-4

© Bill Doherty 2006
© Illustrations on pages 24 and 110: Sheena Reid 2006

All photographs and instances of dogs hunting wild animals in this book,
took place before the implementation of the Hunting Act 2004.

British Library Cataloguing in Publication Data
A catalogue record for this book is available from the British Library.

CONTENTS

ACKNOWLEDGEMENTS

Some of the material for this book has been adapted from articles by the author published in *Countryman's Weekly*.

Special thanks to Elaine Carling, Kevin Hale, Jean Hosey, Joi and Gary Hosker, Bob Perry, wildlife photographer, and Chris Smith for the kind use of their photographs.

This book is dedicated to my late parents

John and Doreen

Always by my side

Scanning the moors

INTRODUCTION

This book endeavours to demonstrate the diversity of true working deerhounds and the hybrids produced from them. It is based on honest opinions, draws from a cornucopia of experience with these dogs and is illustrated through true stories of working them.

Although I am reluctant to vouch for the modern deerhound breed as a whole, I can offer reliable information about the virtues of the Scottish deerhounds in which my father and I became specialists, as well as the first-cross deerhound × greyhounds we produced. I also portray my involvement with deerhound-blooded lurchers spanning a long and memorable period which probably begins before many of this book's readers were born.

I do not remember a time when running dogs did not have a fascination for me. These interests are partly a result of the fact that I emanate from Celtic stock. Inherited traits have been passed from generation to generation along the branches of a family tree that continually produced crops of individuals who kept dogs of some description. In my veins runs the blood of hunters and it is partly due to this ancestry that I am a roamer, constantly lured by the beguiling call of the woods, fields, fells and moors. Total bliss for me lies in having a ceiling of sky over my head, a carpet of soft earth beneath my feet and at least one faithful, canine companion by my side.

Although I deem myself a hunter and sportsman, I also have a great affinity with all wildlife and that Shangri-la we call the countryside. As my life rumbles along the quiet roads and lanes towards its final benediction, I find myself more and more involved with nature, using my skill in bush craft and stealth to seek out and then study all that our fine, rural landscapes have on offer. I possess a prodigious memory and the ability to see and find what others tend to miss and overlook when out in the fields thanks to observational qualities passed to me by my late father, John.

John Doherty and pair of Rohanis deerhounds

Introduction

In his youth my dad kept whippets which he was passionate about racing, travelling by train and bus or even on foot to the racing tracks endemic to every Northumberland pit town and village during the late 1940s and early 1950s. He hunted with these friendly, diminutive sight-hounds in local fields, under the shadows of sulpha-spewing pit-heaps during pre-mixomatosis times.

My father was a joker, a kind of Geordie Mark Twain who had a continuous supply of wise cracks and silly sayings. I remember him facetiously telling me there were so many rabbits during his youth, 100 had to be killed before he could get into a field, and when riding his bike along quiet country lanes, he would have to stop at regular intervals to remove rabbits from the spokes of his wheels.

Time-worn, family photo albums overflowing with sepia-tinted pictures and faded newspaper cuttings boasted of the famous local handicaps won by some of the celebrated dogs he kept. Dog memorabilia of every description always fought for the best places on the walls of my parent's home.

Dad too was very much interested in wildlife and he wouldn't hesitate to take me on slow peregrinations into the fields to find a linnet's nest, to ferret a local, rabbit-infested hedgerow or to sit and observe the darting antics of an electric-blue kingfisher diving into a pool it believed to be its own. His self-taught understanding of basic genetics and various breeding techniques was exceptional. Much of this information was drip fed to me as I accompanied him, and my curiosity about these interests and my craving for greater knowledge grew.

As my affection for dogs became more serious, my first

love remained the lurcher and my father supported me totally along the road to discovery about this breed. I have been so lucky to live in an area of the UK where so many individuals own and hunt with these remarkable dogs, a geographical location also infested with every form of game imaginable which act as foils for dogs, helping them to reach their full potential as workers.

In my early years I was a poacher, as very few local lurcher lads had the luxury of permission to work their dogs on farms. In my case, I didn't want it either. The heart-pounding thrill and excitement of illicit trysts in the countryside with dogs or nets, during the day or while others were fast asleep tucked up in their warm beds, are feelings only true poachers can identify with or experience.

Although my early teens were predominantly taken up with many forms of countryside pursuit, including hunting rabbits and rats with various dogs, I never actually possessed a dog of my own. My first lurcher came much later in life, in the form of a 23½ inch, black, smooth-haired bitch named Bes. She cost me £15, which was considered a king's ransom at the time for a lurcher. But this bitch turned out to be the best all-round lurcher I have owned, or indeed seen, and the sum I paid for her was the best £15 I have ever spent.

Bes' petite phenotype cleverly masked an enormous, internal engine, and the deerhound ancestry in her genotype decreed she would never be one to 'give in'. She was so intelligent; possessing the sensitivity of a dog, but with all the understanding of a human being. From an early age she had the uncanny knack of looking old and would lie meekly on her cosy bed of straw. However, if strong winds, whipped up from the cold waters of the North Sea, began to sing through the bars of her kennel, she would rise like a Phoenix from white-hot ashes and pace the run like a caged lion.

In the fields Bes possessed what I can only describe as outstanding ability. When a quick-footed hare lifted from its form or a rabbit broke from a well-concealed bolt-hole, she would spring into action while other dogs were still day-dreaming. Owning a dog like Bes was like having a clandestine love affair. She gave me so much satisfaction and excitement that I wanted to tell the world, but I had to conceal the fact of her prowess, or indeed existence, for fear of someone taking her from me.

After four years of tremendous service, I mated my constant canine companion with what I perceived to be one of the finest, local, male lurchers of that time: Billy Mercel's gypsy-bred dog, Paddy. This rough-haired, black-and-tan dog had old fashioned, bob-tailed collie in his breeding and, although I have never been a lover of the inconsistency associated with border collie crosses, such undesirable traits are rarely manifest with beardy composites, especially those bred from genuine working stock.

Paddy was one of the hardest lurchers I have seen. To say he completely annihilated foxes would be an understatement. He had a particular aversion to dogs larger than himself (especially Alsatians for some reason) and, although he never actually went looking for a scrap, he wouldn't allow another dog to put one over on him.

From this well-planned union, I retained a black, rough-coated bitch – a most adorable lurcher that was so eager to please and just loved to be cuddled. Kit was extremely fast and agile and, although many of the men with whom I hunted thought her to be the tightest bitch they had seen, I had the advantage of making the comparison with her mother, Bes, when she was in her prime. In that competition, Kit would always have to take a close second place.

Kit stood 24 inches at the shoulders. She was a demon when hunting larger quarry such as roe deer and fox, but fickle on rabbits, where sometimes she would and other times she wouldn't. Whenever she grew stale or tired of the repetitive run after run on large numbers of coney when lamping, I would take her on an outing where her strength and aggression took precedence over her fleetness of foot. This ploy would once again set her up in good stead to accompany me into areas where we always wreaked havoc on large rabbit populations. At this point, I believed Bes and Kit to be the best two lurchers that I have worked as a pair at any one time, and very few strong, northern hares would escape their joint abilities.

Kit was barren and never came into season. Just like the formidable tally of quarry she was establishing, her hunting reputation quickly grew and this was to be my downfall, and hers. I had done a first-class job in protecting my bitch, Bes, from birth to retirement, but I wasn't to be so fortunate with Kit. She was stolen in 1990. Through much detective work, I eventually found out who the local thieves were, and I delivered retribution in such a way that they haven't realised to this day. But I never saw my beloved bitch again.

To continue my line, and to follow an astute breeding plan devised by my father, I obtained a black, bitch pup from a litter sired by Cap, one of Kit's litter brothers. Cap was a very useful all-round lurcher. He could course and take hare, fox and roe deer single-handedly, and although not as experienced in taking large numbers of rabbits as lurchers from my kennel, he always got his fair share. Cap remained a constant element in a kennel where his owner unceremoniously culled anything that didn't come up to scratch.

I called the bitch pup I obtained Yella. She was a re-incarnation of her grandmother, Bes: the same colour, similar marking and the same physical dimensions. Partly because of her genotype, she was one of the top lamping bitches in mid to north Northumberland for a long time. This lurcher that just couldn't be sickened accounted for over 50 rabbits in a night's graft on more than 30 occa-sions. People hunting with me were amazed at this little bitch's stamina and efficiency in catching rabbits. I kept Yella solely for the hunting of this humble quarry, both on the lamp and during the day, so it is perhaps of no sur-prise that she accounted for less than 20 hares and only a handful of roe deer in a working career lasting over 12 years.

I bred a number of litters from Yella using various male lurchers that I deemed worthy, all of which possessed an amount of deerhound in their breeding. The best puppy was probably Sophie, a blue bitch that I originally kept back for myself, sired by Blue, another of Billy Mercel's outstanding all rounders. I later passed this pup on as a favour to a very good friend of mine, Kevin Hale from Bedlington in Northumberland. Kevin was keen, and his raw enthusiasm reminded me much of my own when I was his age. Such a blend of pure passion, dedication and a well-bred dog saw Kevin take Sophie into pole position in the local lurcher world for many years, with nothing locally able to match her as a taker of exceptional numbers of rabbits.

This little blue bitch, at the time of writing, still holds the record tally of 81 rabbits taken on one night's work with the lamp in the mid-Northumberland area! On the same night this phenomenal haul was taken, her mother Yella, at the ripe old age of eight took 80. Sophie also accounted for two hares on that same outing, a formidable, unbeaten record indeed. I consider myself extremely lucky to have been part of such a spectacle.

Yella was a lurcher that fed a very hungry part of me. She was the last dog that I truly loved, and I would never hide the fact that I shed a river of tears when she passed away. From the final run this bitch made, I never allowed myself to become so attached to any dog again.

In 1991, my father and I decided to branch into keeping a breed both of us had admired for many years. But it appeared to be as difficult to land a Scottish deerhound as it was to launch a rocket to the moon. Then, after a lot of searching and knock-backs by some uncooperative, opinioned 'ladies' associated with the breed, we eventually obtained a male deerhound, Shenval Isidore, also called Thorn. This one-year-old dog was slightly underweight when we obtained him, but thanks to my father's experience he was built up, and through a joint effort was coached into becoming a decent hunter and potent stud dog.

As a stud dog, Thorn followed in the footsteps of his famous father, Shenval Druid, and his virginity was lost to an Irish-bred greyhound bitch when he was only 15 months, resulting in a litter of 10 brindle puppies. Many male deerhounds have had their libido bred out of them, just as much as they have their hunting instinct. So they are not, shall we say, the sexiest dogs in the world; some find it difficult to raise even their heads when a bitch fully in season is presented to them. Thorn would never be classed as a considerate lover, and there was no gentle fore-play in his bedroom manner. He would sniff his intended, practically throw her in the air and be tied before you could say, 'Where's the Vaseline?' This male deerhound sired well over 200 progeny in his time with us, some pure-bred deerhounds, the rest deerhound × greyhound hybrids.

The deerhound bug bit hard and to satisfy our enthusiasm we obtained Gwen (Rosslyn Fling), a gorgeous, well-bred bitch from Brian Doak, a breeder in Northern Ireland. Brian's Rosslyn breed of deerhounds impressed us each time we visited the championship shows, either exhibiting or on reconnaissance missions. I also monitored how a number of dogs produced from his lines fared very well at the hare-coursing meetings organised by the English Deerhound Club, even though Brian himself wasn't an active follower of the chase. The breeding of our newly-acquired Rosslyn bitch also matched our Shenval dog's *pie de grue* very well. With such a quality, genetically-matched foundation bitch, our Doxhope deerhounds kennel was established.

A mating between Thorn and Gwen produced nine healthy puppies. We kept two for ourselves, Doxhope Laird of Ashpark (Lewis) and Doxhope Lady Annadaille (Meg). We also bought back another bitch a couple of years later, Doxhope Ambecky (Becky), a bitch that had slipped the net so to speak – just going to show how anyone can get assessing pups wrong.

My dad was always interested in showing dogs, seeing it as 'the window of your kennel', and his most famous Shetland sheepdog, Rupert (Doxburn Cavalier), has left his mark in the history of that particular breed. We dabbled for a while in exhibiting our stock but found a lot of the windows, as well as all the doors, closed and well and truly locked.

All our exhibited deerhounds actually did manage to qualify for Crufts at various times, but we were becoming disillusioned as the size of the show-orientated types escalated to Irish wolfhound proportions – this is not what my father and I wanted in our stock. We were not prepared to be followers of show trends: we were dog men, not bleating sheep.

Exaggerated show points were bringing in faults at an alarming rate; shortcomings and structural faults that wouldn't get better or disappear with age and that would be found out in the field of work, even if deliberately ignored in the show arena. More emphasis was being put on ear carriage and coat than on soundness. It was also so disappointing to be told accurately beforehand at three different championship shows which deerhound was going to win – but not, may I add, through merit. Such goings-on to me are tantamount to cheating, and after that third event we never showed again. 'Showing is a mug's game,' I can remember my father angrily telling me.

At Doxhope Deerhounds my father and I took great pleasure in producing sound stock. Our hounds were lighter framed than those in the show arena during the late 90s, but we were producing what we wanted. Our stock resembled the type and proportions of deerhounds from bygone days often depicted in old books and manuscripts when the showground for these formidable ancestors was heather-clad, Scottish hillsides, their prize a red deer hind or stag. More importantly, our dogs performed like them.

Dad and I always worked on the premise that deer-hounds are not beasts of burden and do not pull carts. Our kennel rarely faced hefty vet bills or our working stock serious injuries, and we acquired good numbers of puppies per litter. We received hundreds of enquiries for our pups each year, and the main question was always, 'Your dogs aren't those wolf-hound types, are they?' They certainly were not!

Any advertising costs were as minute as our vet's bills. All the hounds we bred and kept worked towards their keep. They hunted all legal British quarry. We also ex-

Joi Hosker with AKC Champion, Doxhope Lustre

ported deerhounds to America, Germany and Southern Ireland.

During 2002, we wound down our deerhound-breeding programs as my father's health began to fail. We still produced the occasional litter and also some deerhound × greyhounds, right up to my dad's death on December 13, 2002. I was hit so hard by his death that I immediately sold everything we had so painstakingly built up and became a virtual recluse in the hunting-dog world we had both loved so much.

I have never truly got over what was the greatest loss I have suffered in my lifetime, but there is now light at the end of the tunnel and who knows what the future will bring. In 2006, an example from our breed, Doxhope Lustre, owned by Gary and Joi Hosker, was made up into an American Kennel Club champion – a fact that my late father would have been very proud of indeed – and was a testimony to his endeavours.

It took us many years of hard work to obtain a good name in producing quality, working deerhounds and their hybrids. And that name was, and always will be, Doxhope Deerhounds.

CHAPTER I

WORKING DEERHOUNDS

The Scottish deerhound type has remained comparatively constant for over 1,000 years. While most other things have changed during the same period, the deerhound seems to have been forgotten somehow, as though some form of Brigadoon spell had been cast upon it.

Many of the journals and manuscripts detailing its long history are well known for their accounts of the hound's type, origins and hunting prowess. Only a few authors in modern times, however, have highlighted the deerhound's working virtues and abilities; in each case the subject has only been touched upon, and none has concentrated on the deerhound solely as a working dog.

More recent books seem to have been cloned and all of them concentrate on the history of specific kennels, on individual show champions or their owners, and the field has become stagnant and readers bored by such repetition. Many of the accounts are personal brags or advertisements for friends, and the aim of making others more aware of the virtues of such a wonderful dog has been lost.

Before the first English, organised dog show at Newcastle upon Tyne in Northumberland in 1859, the deerhound had existed solely for work or companionship, and many famous individuals owned examples of the breed that in many cases immortalised some of the vir-

The red deer, the Scottish deerhound's traditional quarry

tues of the Scottish deerhound.

The blue touch paper that was to rocket the hound into the theatre of exhibitions was lit, however, and the deerhound was included in dog shows from 1860 onwards. Since then, the dog has adapted, not only to a world of rosettes and challenge certificates, but also to the quarry species legally available for it to hunt.

Over the decades, a small number of dedicated breeders and owners have strived to retain the hound as a dual-purpose dog, for both show and work. Yet before the Hunting Act of 2004 in England and Wales, not many of these enthusiasts would have had the opportunity to work their deerhounds on its traditional prey. The majority settled for legal, less aristocratic adversaries, such as fox, hare and even the unassuming rabbit.

Before the hunting with dogs act eventually came into force, it was one of the English Deerhound Club's aims to ensure that those members wishing to work their hounds had the opportunity to do so and, to give the club its due, they did organise many events during the hunting seasons. At organised coursing competitions, hares with their remarkable agility served to keep the dog fit and active, while maintaining its desire for the chase. The hunting of these animals was then outlawed and, at the time of writing, the humble rabbit is the only remaining legal target for the Scottish deerhound.

The majority of post-millennium deerhounds are more accustomed to show rings than to craggy mountainsides where eagles and buzzards soar on motionless wings, heather-clad hills that echo the grouse's strident call, grass fields or rough fells guarded by diving pewits

Coursing deerhounds on the Fens

and circling curlews. Most will never know what it is like to gallop over any of these terrains with the ghosts of their ancestors looking down on them with keen, applauding eyes.

In my opinion there is a definite working type of deerhound (even if some devotees of the breed bemoan the fact), a dog quite separate from the show deerhound – and not only in appearance. A house sparrow that sometimes nests in a tree is not a tree sparrow, and working deerhounds are not giant show dogs trying, now and then, to fulfil the whims of their owners; they are dogs purposely bred for work, to fit what is for many the proper mould of the deerhound, which, although not smashed, is rather cracked.

Currently, there is not the volume of people with an interest in the hound's working qualities necessary to maintain them and, if fashion or the inability to breed to, or interpret, the breed standard continues to take precedence, the deerhound's true type will be lost forever.

WHAT IS A STANDARD?
The standard for the Scottish deerhound was based around the dog's original function, to hunt deer, and was originally born out of the need to document desirable points, so that the hound's quality and function remained as consistent as possible for future generations.

If we were to imagine that the deerhound was in some way an endangered species, it might be easier to appreciate why a documented breed type is necessary. Breeders have a huge responsibility to adhere to such a standard, basically so that the deerhound along with its characteristics never becomes extinct. Although the written standard for the Scottish deerhound exists for this reason, many modern show deerhounds do not live up to it, and in reality it has become quite irrelevant.

If a hound possesses all the aesthetic finishing touches required in today's show deerhound, but does not have the desire or ability to chase, it is not correct according to the breed standard. We can look at it another way: if the standard were likened to a design-guide for a sports car, but an engineer built the car without its engine, it would not really be a functional sports car.

A true working-type deerhound should closely resemble the original standard and, because of this, would probably never suit the modern show trend of size taking precedence. Gargantuan show specimens with their exaggerated points will rarely, if ever, emulate the soundness, health or working abilities of the various working deerhounds which, as the breed standard states, 'should resemble a rough-coated greyhound of larger bone and size'. It is surprising how many people involved with the breed get a little mixed up with the aesthetic differences between a greyhound and an Irish wolfhound.

The original breed standard states that the size of a bitch should be no smaller than 28 inches and a dog no less than 30 inches, and early documented accounts show that working deerhounds that were doing what they were designed to do were around this height, possibly smaller. No mention is made of upper limits in the breed standard, so that a fit and active, well-put-together, 29-inch deerhound male that pulls red deer hinds down consistently has become undesirable, while a 35-inch, 120lb-plus, cow-hocked male that wouldn't

Female roe deer

chase a deer if it ran past its nose is what the show frater-nity now wants.

Had the standard stipulated that, say, more than two inches above the required heights was 'highly undesirable', we would see a far better quality deerhound on the show bench, with fewer of the original functional properties bred out.

WORKING DEERHOUNDS ON DEER

When it was legal to do so, the only species of deer I had the opportunity to hunt with my hounds was the roe deer, *Capreolus capreolus*.

Roe deer are one of only two species of deer that are considered to be indigenous to the British Isles, the other being the red deer. Remains identified as roe have been found in Britain dating back to 400,000 BC.

These deer are classed as smallish, with adult males be-tween 24 and 27 inches in height at the shoulders and weighing anything up to just over 60lbs. I have taken many of what I would class as good specimens with my dogs, carcasses that when prepared and ready for the game dealer (gutted, skin on, head and lower legs removed) weighed over 40lbs, with one particular adult male topping the scales at 46lbs.

A roe deer is a fairly fast and fleet animal and is a mixture of craftiness and utter stupidity when being chased by a dog. It is an incredible jumper and it uses this agile trait to escape its pursuer whenever it can. A good working-type deerhound can come to terms with the creature's speed and agility on open ground but, once a chase branches off into the sanctuary of a plantation, very few are taken by dogs. This deer can cut through these wooded settings like a hot knife through butter.

Over the years, I have often witnessed deerhounds seizing roe that had been 'worked out' from plantations, woods or copses. This consists of one or two people walking slowly through the trees, clapping their hands or tapping tree-trunks in order to drive out any deer present in a given direction. The hounds are positioned outside the wood, and, when a roe emerges into the field, it is allowed a fairly lengthy lift, so that it has no chance to turn back and re-enter the wood, and the deerhounds are slipped.

Without doubt, the most effective technique of taking roe deer with deerhounds is at night with the aid of a high-powered lamp. Under the cloak of darkness, shy roe deer surface from the trees and hiding places to feed. A hunter that has done his homework can follow a plantation edge and shine out into the deer's favourite fields of peas, turnips, young rape or stubble-fields cut a few weeks before and that now boast a growth of young tender grass shoots.

Roe deer rely mainly on their finely-tuned senses of smell and hearing. If the approaching hunter has the wind in his face, so that any noise or scent is masked, he can get relatively close to his quarry before the deerhound is released. A deer in this situation will look towards the light, straining to see what is going on, its head moving to and fro, virtually unaware that a dog is approaching.

Even if a deerhound is slipped at a greater distance from a roe on the lamp, it should have no problem in coming to terms with the deer as far as speed is concerned, as long as the creature is not allowed to enter any nearby wood.

Roe deer are the most wide-spread species of deer in Great Britain, making them the most likely deer most hounds would ever get to chase. A deerhound running roe will pull out all the stops and very little training is required. The scent of a deer carried on the wind will trigger off an attack of frenzied excitement – it is as if the dog senses this is why he's here: these are the creatures he was designed to hunt. But it is not just a matter of how a deerhound gets to its prey, there is also the question of the method the dog uses to take it.

The deerhounds I have worked never mess about when running roe deer. As soon as there is a chance of a strike, the hound takes it. Most deer are hit with such force that they are either bundled over or thrown into the air. Most deerhounds latch on to a back leg while others I have seen run alongside the deer and pull the creature down by the neck.

When legal, hunting roe deer with dogs was never my main interest. But whenever I had the opportunity to do so, on the invitation of a gamekeeper or with the permission of the landowner, I always jumped at the chance. In all my time, I have never witnessed a roe deer get up once pulled down by one of my Scottish deerhounds.

WORKING DEERHOUNDS ON FOX

Although deerhounds by dint of their nature and excellent temperaments are usually tolerant of smaller animals, this does not extend to the red fox, *Vulpes vulpes*, and nearly all deerhounds have a particular dislike of this chicken thief. Even the most placid hound that has not yet embarked on any form of hunting foray will snarl and bare its teeth in any close encounter of the fox kind.

The red fox is widely distributed throughout the British Isles. Once a creature of the countryside, he now finds solace in our towns and cities. The sexes are very much alike,

A vixen with cub

although the vixen is usually smaller and sometimes has a shorter, greyer coat.

The life cycle of the fox begins early in the year, when a single litter of between three and eight cubs is born. In the northerly county of Northumberland where I live, this breeding activity takes place in March or April; in southern counties, litters can be produced even earlier. The months during which foxes whelp usually coincide with the lambing storms, a busy period for the farmer, a time that provides Mr and Mrs Fox with a ready supply of easy meat to rear their offspring. A fox's appetite for new-born lambs should never be in doubt: they will wantonly kill far in excess of their requirements when trying to provide nourishment for their cubs.

While temporarily employed on various Northumbrian hill farms over the years, I have witnessed at first-hand the carnage caused by foxes at lambing time. On one farm close to the Scottish border at the beginning of 1997, no less than 50 lambs were taken by fox. A couple of us, armed with deerhounds and lurchers, set to work at night with the aid of lamps to rid the area of its *vulpus* problem. Seven foxes were killed over three nights' work, but it was not till the seventh and final fox was taken out that this particular flock was safe.

Young foxes are born into the world blind and are suckled inside the earth for about a month. The female fox is a model parent, cat-like in her approach to motherhood. After the first four weeks, the vixen will fetch food to the earth for the cubs to consume, usually small rodents.

These earths are rarely dug by the fox – they prefer to squat in the homes of badgers or rabbits and, in a lot of these cases, I have seen them close all but one entrance to their chosen residence. If the vixen is disturbed in any way, she will have no hesitation in moving her family to a new location.

Foxes are in the main nocturnal hunters, creatures of the dark that normally lie up through the day. Their guile is proverbial, and countless instances of the fox's cunning and slyness have been documented over the years. Apart from the killing of lambs, the fox's dietary habits also include the taking of fowl, both of which help to ensure he is persecuted by farmers and landowners alike.

I was never a miner, and spade and shovel at my time of life now fill me with dread, so the digging out of foxes holed up in a stop does not light my Davey lamp, although in my younger days I could be found on the occasional dig. My experience of hunting fox with my dogs is confined mostly to lamping, and a typical season's tally would be around 50. The majority of encounters with foxes occurred when I was out with the lamp in search of rabbits, hares or roe deer. A fox appearing in my beam has always been classed as a legitimate target, and a night's sport has sometimes begun with my deerhounds killing two or three foxes. If there was a chance of chasing a fox on the lamp I would always take it, and deerhounds have enough strength and stamina to do this without spoiling the rest of the night's work through tiredness or injury.

Young foxes are fairly straightforward and are excellent for bringing on young dogs; they are fairly easy meat for any working deerhound matched against them and unlikely to cause their pursuer any serious damage. These foxes are uneducated to the dangers lurking behind the swishing, dancing light in front of them. They are lured to a suitable distance by the hunter 'squeaking' or with a call made for the purpose, or by the tempting squeals of a rabbit already caught by the dog, and the eager deerhound is slipped. Older, more experienced foxes can be brought into closer positions by various squeaking techniques too, but they are more formidable opponents than the youngsters and they can and do bite back.

My working deerhounds weigh 70 to 80lbs, depending on gender. In America such dogs might be used to take coyote, in Australia kangaroo, just as the ancestors of the modern deerhound killed wolves – a phenomenal achievement for any dog. Adult British red foxes are therefore totally outmatched by a single working deerhound.

WORKING DEERHOUNDS ON HARE

During the Iron Age, hares were kept as pets and, because of their speed, it was thought that they were used by the gods

A brown hare

as messengers. A hare would be let free to run and the direction it took was used to foretell the future.

The brown hare, *Lepus europaeus*, is the ultimate prey of pure-bred deerhounds or of any deerhound composite. A hare will not bite back like a fox, she will never plough a fence down when being pursued like a red stag and she won't clear a fence, hedge or dry-stone wall like a roe. But what a hare will do is put the top running dogs in their place, break the heart or burst the lungs of a sapling that should not be on her back, and at times give dogs a right good showing-up in the process with her speed, agility and stamina.

It was 18 February 2005 when the 2004 Hunting Act came into force. Of all the hunting pastimes affected by that piece of legislation, it was the banning of coursing hares with dogs that caused me such discontentment. Hunting deer was never my favourite sporting pastime, and I was in no way an enthusiastic follower of any pack hunting. But watching a strong hare in front of a good dog on a tilled field, with clouds of fine brown earth thrown up on every turn is an exciting spectacle, and just thinking about some of the great courses I have witnessed still sends goose bumps down my neck.

Although the brown hare is a member of the double-toothed rodent family, sub order *duplicidentata*, its body is designed to run: it has fantastic speed and incredible endurance; its vertebrae are long, giving it power and suppleness; it has a large chest that houses massive lungs for maximum intake of air; it has five clawed toes on its front feet and four on its back feet, and its soles are cushioned with fur – the result: a pure, unadulterated running machine.

The sexes are alike, but it is said that the buck has a slightly smaller body, shorter head and redder shoulders. Hares are widely distributed in Great Britain, but less so on high hills and moors, and can be found virtually anywhere that is under cultivation. Some authorities believe that hare now breed all year round, and during my wanderings I must admit I have observed leverets in almost every month of the year, but the main courting season for hares is February–March, possibly a little later in Scotland.

The hare can produce two to five young, and these are born covered with hair, open-eyed and are able to run immediately. They are fully independent at a month old. Leverets resemble the adults, albeit in miniature form. Young females can breed from between eight and 12 months of age, and can produce three to four broods a year. Hares do not pair up permanently.

Adult hares are, in the main, unsociable, solitary creatures. They select a convenient place (form) and, if necessary, can spend all day crouched in it. These forms are chosen to give maximum view, or to have shade, sun or shelter, depending on the weather conditions.

Athletic hares have been known to jump a five-foot high wall, they are good swimmers and will cross wide rivers to elude pursuers or reach a favourite pasture. They are wholly vegetarian and can be particularly destructive in spring-time, eating any tender young shoots.

Its sense of smell and its hearing are acute, but it cannot see straight ahead owing to the position of its eyes. When hunted, the hare possesses all the cunning of a fox, with an array of tricks up its sleeve such as making long, sideways leaps to mask its scent. However, its limited vision and the fact that it is a creature of habit makes it an easy animal to snare and net.

The hare's survival in Great Britain is largely due to its being protected for sport, so the 2004 Hunting Act will have far reaching effects on the hare population, as it allows shooting hares, but not hare coursing, the activity for which the protection given was mostly intended. Shooting is indiscriminate and culls even the strongest, while coursing tends to weed out the weak – the stronger, fitter hares escaping to breed again.

It will be interesting to see how well this magnificent creature fares over the coming decades, as farmers and landowners are still allowed to kill hares because of destruction to their crops. Perhaps hare-drives, in which large numbers of hares are shot, will become ever more popular. I was once invited to such a shoot – although, because of my dislike of them, I had to borrow a gun. On the first day, 305 hares were slaughtered and, on the second, another 308 were killed from more or less the same area. It seems that the powers that be concede the need for some sort of hare control as long as hunters go about it with guns.

The average deerhound does not have the ability to catch a brown hare, unless the creature is too old, too young, has been picked up out of its seat or makes a fundamental mistake in its get-away plan – in other words, only if it is a fluke. Some of the large show hounds would have as much success against a hare as a Pomeranian would. A good, working-type deerhound, however, will catch hares, but many will only end up exercising their quarry.

The Doxhope deerhounds that I consider to have been our best – Becky, Gwen and Meg – were all capable of taking hares, not just hares in fen and moorland, but those of my native Northumberland and those indigenous to the Scottish Borders and beyond. Hares in these latter, harsher geographical locations are just as athletic as those in Lincolnshire. However, they are raced in small fields and pastures, so it takes a sharper, more determined type of dog to take them regularly, dogs that rely on speed, stamina and agility, rather than on stamina alone.

Although this trio was capable of catching hares, they could never have matched the hare-catching qualities of a good lurcher or longdog. Nevertheless, they gave me a great deal of pleasure watching their determined performances.

While I have worked deerhounds, I have hunted hare both in the daytime and at night with the lamp. My records for each deerhound I worked suggest that more hares were taken at night, but this is as expected, as there are many more opportunities in darkness. A daylight foray may only see one or two courses, whereas at night dogs can race up to double figures, if the location is right and if they are fit enough.

An important contributing factor that aids success is striking ability, which working deerhounds usually possess in varying degrees. They certainly have enough speed and the stamina required to stay with the hare until an opportunity arises to take it. But it is their striking ability that determines whether they can make a kill and avoid a longer course or whether the hare escapes.

Although the working deerhound possesses more than enough stamina to be successful against the average hare, he may not have the renowned staying power of his Arabian cousin, the saluki. Nevertheless, the deerhound puts a lot of physical effort into getting up to its quarry, while the saluki tends to run behind its prey, pacing it, so that it could seemingly carry on running forever. Hares run by a deerhound, on the other hand, are worked and pressed into mistakes.

Speed is an obvious feature that any dog must possess if it is to catch such an athlete as the brown hare. There is much debate as to exactly how fast a hare can run. Some writers believe this to be in the region of 35mph, but I have clocked a hare on the road with my car's odometer at 40mph, so I know the estimate of 35mph is too low. No deerhound can match such a speed, but what the dog does have is a deceptive running style: its long legs may not be able to emulate the rapid ground-smacking technique of a whippet, but their lengthy strides have the capacity to cover distances at a phenomenal rate, and a good example of a working-type deerhound mimics to some degree the head-down-bottom-up running style of the greyhound.

THE BLUE OR MOUNTAIN HARE

The blue or mountain hare, *Lepus timidus*, or *maigheach-bhàn* as it is called in Gaelic, is not as strong an animal as its brown cousin, and is certainly no match whatsoever for any deerhound of working type. This limited ability and the fact that the hares are found in areas that suit the deerhound's running style ensure the dog is victor in the great majority of chases.

Although the blue hare is softer in some ways than the brown hare, it lives in a much harsher environment compared to where the brown is mostly found. It is an animal of upland, heather moorland, and the largest pockets are usually found on higher moors managed for grouse shooting. The controlled burning of these environments produces different growths of heather that are ideal for both hare and grouse.

To combat the hostile winter weather found on these moors, blue hares possess a woollier coat than the brown. This fur turns white at certain times of the year, for camouflage. This change of colour can vary and some individuals never turn fully white. The tips of the ears stay black.

The average size of the mountain hare is smaller than that of the brown hare. I have tasted both at the table and would say that blue hare meat is inferior and not as pleasant, but still quite edible when slowly cooked in a casserole along with onions, mushrooms and black pudding.

Many authorities propose that there have been cases of hybridisation between the species, and suggest that such happenings may threaten the blue hare's genetic diversity, although to what extent is still to be determined.

While the average deerhound may not possess the ability to match the pace, agility and sheer stamina of a fit brown hare, the same deerhound will most probably take blue hares with consistency. Not only have I witnessed such pure deerhounds killing these creatures, I have also seen poorer examples of lurchers catching blues, dogs that could never take brown hares as long as they had a wagging tail. So in my estimation, these hares are fairly easy, so much so that I have never added any I have taken to my dog's main overall record of achievements, although I know of many lurchermen who have.

In those grand times not so long ago, when hare coursing was a legitimate sporting pastime with little or no interference from town-bred politicians looking for a new, vote-catching bandwagon to jump on, both the English Deerhound Club and the Saluki Club went some way to make certain their members had sport for their dogs on hares. Coursing sub-committees of both clubs staged well-organised events that helped ensure that the respective breeds were kept as workers, while maintaining a strong hare populace on the moors and arable terrain where they hunted.

I have had the great pleasure to have coursed with both deerhounds and salukis against blue hares at events on various moors in Scotland, but I would have to say I much prefer the workman-like style of the deerhounds, as the playful salukis tend to try my patience, with more time being spent trying to get the hare off them, than as a spectator to a good course.

On private visits to the same moors, I have always attained good results with my deerhounds. Gwen, Becky and Meg have all accounted for double-figured tallies on a day's sport. Gwen and Meg were very determined killers of blue hares – Becky, well, she was something else. She would have been a formidable match for most lurchers in the country on this quarry where numbers were the order of the day.

The blue hare would never have been classed as the ultimate quarry for the working deerhound, but it is a creature that gave some good accounts, and helped, through legal sport at the time, to ensure the deerhound breed was kept fit and active.

WORKING DEERHOUNDS ON RABBITS

A good friend of mine, the late Brian Plummer, along with Les White, used to coach me in my crude, early writing attempts during the mid-90s, and an elemental rule the great man constantly drove into me was that my writings should always be factually correct. Of the less accurate statements I have heard tell or have seen written in various magazines – one that never fails to annoy me – is that deerhounds are too big to catch rabbits. The proponents of such inept thinking may have imagined some gargantuan, show-winning deerhound when they made such a sweeping statement; they certainly didn't have mine or any other working-type deerhound in mind.

The rabbit, *Oryctolagus cuniculus*, is said to be found wherever there is grass and is certainly found in virtually every part of Great Britain, from moors to fields, from parks to gardens, even our motorway sidings are strewn with a continuous supply of feeding coney.

Rabbit fossils have been found in various countries dating back 30 to 40 million years. The original name was in fact coney, and the name rabbit was actually the name used to refer to a baby coney. Kittens and kits were adopted later as names for the young of the rabbit. When first introduced to the British Isles, it was thought that rabbits would not be able to withstand the hostile winters, so they were kept in large open enclosures.

A breeding stock known as 'clapper coneys' were held in reserve, housed in hutches. Of these, some were kept as pets and were known as 'sweethearts'.

The sexes of rabbits are very much alike, but the bucks have shorter and rounder shaped heads. The meat of the rabbit has been used for centuries for the table, and the fur utilized for clothing and was once dyed to imitate other, more fashionable furs. The felt used in millinery was always rabbit fur, four pelts being needed to make one hat.

In favourable conditions in the wild, a female rabbit can have four to eight broods per year, and these can consist of three to nine young each, with maximum litter numbers probably occurring in June. Unlike the young of the hare, rabbits are born into the world naked, blind and with ears closed. They are, however, very rapid developers and can run at 14 days and are self-supporting within a month. If a rabbit doesn't become an unfortunate, road-side casualty, or isn't taken by one of the many predators that find it so attractive, it can live for seven to eight years. Akin to hares, rabbits seem to breed all year round.

Rabbits tend to spend most of their day underground, coming out in early morning and at night-fall to feed. In certain more secluded areas, however, they live in thick cover such as bracken, gorse or turnips etc. The rabbit has many enemies, such as man, stoats and weasels and birds of prey, but a really severe winter can do as much as any of these to reduce rabbit numbers.

As a quarry species, the rabbit has been the main sport for many contemporary, running dog enthusiasts, including myself. I have employed many hunting techniques over the years to take the creature, including ferreting and nocturnal long-netting, and I have even been employed in a semi-professional capacity to gas rabbits. Of all the methods available, it is with running dogs that I find greatest satisfaction, including with my deerhounds, which I allow to take part in all the hunting disciplines I would a lurcher or longdog.

My working of deerhounds on rabbits can be classes into three main categories, lamping, ferreting and general mooching about.

Lamping is probably the most effective of this trio, and the improvement with which this hunting form has blessed lurcherdom can also be bestowed on the deerhounds of any owner wishing to use it. Lamping allows the hunter the opportunity to pursue many more rabbits in a short period of time, far more than with any daylight sport. Deerhounds quickly learn what is expected of them when the light is shone in the darkness, and they absolutely love it. A deerhound worked regularly on the lamp possesses the intelligence and sagacity to become competent: looking down the beam with keen eyes, picking up squatting rabbits when the chance arises and, if hunted in areas where large numbers of this pest are found, the dog will account for some really good bags. In places where my lurchers have taken 30 to 40 plus, my deerhounds have taken rabbit numbers in the high 20s.

All my deerhounds have worked in conjunction with ferrets and, as with lamping, they really enjoy ferreting days out. Deerhounds are intelligent and it doesn't take them long to work out what to look and listen for, where to stand and that the musky-smelling creature that keeps disappearing and re-appearing from holes in the ground are friends not foe. When sport is slow, however, they become bored and whine impatiently, but this passes quickly once a rabbit bolts.

Walking moors and fells, where the grazing is partially hidden by patches of spiny grass, with dogs free running in front of me is an activity I truly relish. I am fortunate in this respect living in close proximity to the Scottish borders, time-forgotten lands ideal for this pastime. As I tread this history-steeped ground, any accompanying deerhounds put all their hunting instincts into overdrive as they search for scents to excite or an explosion of fur to chase. A jaunt here is rarely measured by the hour; once I escape the shackles of tedium, I am away all day, getting well and truly caught up in my surroundings, sometimes returning in complete darkness, my belt heavily laden with rabbits. Over such periods of time on the land, deerhounds, although never fully tested, do a fair amount of work and, if the distance they have run and walked could be measured, it would be formidable indeed.

THE WORKING DEERHOUND: THE FINAL ANALYSIS

In this chapter I have given an insight into and my opinion of the working deerhound's capabilities when hunting a variety of game. I have used various references from the deerhound's lengthy past, the original breed standard and comparisons between those deerhounds that work and those that play. I have also included information about the hunting prowess of those deerhounds my father and I specialised in, a working breed. I have highlighted precisely and accurately what our dogs were capable of, and only with quarry I have had experience of hunting. When I say these deerhounds can do something, the reader can rest assured that the dogs have actually done it.

An anthology of true hunting stories
using my deerhounds

CHAPTER 2

BLUE HARES AND PURPLE HILLS

With the working deerhound kennels of Doxhope firmly established, my father, John, and I were now reaping the benefits of having established a good name as producers of sound deerhound stock – a reputation earned not through clever advertising or self-praise, but through word of mouth, recommendations from those who had either obtained dogs from us or who had seen examples of our strain and liked what they saw.

No one could argue that our deerhounds truly fitted the descriptions of hounds of old, when they were primarily working dogs, hunting not only their traditional quarry, the formidable red deer, but also fallow deer and fox. More recent times have witnessed the deerhound adapting to smaller adversaries for sport, including the athletic hare, and we had geared our breeding programme partly to cope with this and, of course, any other legitimate quarry too.

In all my involvement with hare coursing at both public and private events, the 1998 season, when the results of our breeding plans had much success at all levels, is one that holds some of the fondest memories for me.

As the usual ambassador of Château Doxhope on such occasions, I was able to observe deerhounds from many different kennels and breeding and of various shapes and sizes, all pitting their wits and running abilities against the fit and healthy stock of well-maintained coursing grounds. These outings also acted as reconnaissance missions, scouting opportunities to find potential stud dogs for our bitches, at the

A group of enthusiasts watching a course

same time allowing me the opportunity to witness some of the most beautiful, and in some cases unique, geographical locations of Britain.

It was during this late-1990s campaign that our eldest Scottish deerhound bitch, Gwen, was entered in what was to be the third meeting of the season – the second staged in Scotland on heather – against that plucky adversary, the mountain hare.

Coursing this quarry on such hostile running terrain has always been one of my favourite sporting activities. Not necessarily because the blue hare is any less of an opponent than its stronger brown cousin, but more because I delight in visiting such unspoilt areas – havens for wildlife and steeped in folklore – where I can watch deerhounds performing, even if not against their traditional prey, over ground they are designed to cover well.

Initially, poor weather threatened any ideas we may have had of enjoying our weekend away, but luck was finally on our side, and the pouring rain subsided into a gentle drizzle. Bird and beast, with a shake of feather or fur, began to emerge from their hidden retreats as sunshine broke through the clouds and the countryside came alive.

We now found ourselves bathed in wintry sunshine, as we left our quaint hotel in the time-forgotten village of Gifford for the coursing grounds and the purple-capped hills in the distance. As we journeyed, a number of red grouse raised their heads to stare intently at the travelling party. High above us common buzzards soared, taking full advantage of thermals that swirled invisibly between the land and sky. Charms of tiny goldfinches acted as our escorts, dancing like nymphs and dryads between purple-plumed cotton-thistles strewn along the narrow roadside.

After several dry weeks, the torrent of rain had swollen the stream that ran alongside the winding track. Its tumbling waters drew salmon and sea trout back to the spawning beds in which their life cycle had begun. Drew, the head gamekeeper, who lived with his family in the hills, knew everything there was to know about what went on between the banks of the burn and had been keeping a watchful eye out for the migratory fish.

'Ach, they've been here in large numbers for a few weeks now,' he told us, which explained why they were losing their colourful and well-fed appearance and instead beginning to look rather drab and slender.

Drew also told us he had seen a lot of blue hares, more than usual for the time of the year. A helpful gamekeeper with such intimate knowledge of the terrain and its creatures is a godsend to an event such as this and is well worth his weight in Glenfiddich. As a result, we were all hoping for two days of exciting, well-organised sport.

The assembled group of spectators

On reaching our destination, concealed deep within the rolling hills, Kenneth Cassels introduced the judge, Peter Mosey and slipper, Darren Balloch to the group. Mr Cassels was the founder of organised hare coursing with pure-bred, Kennel Club-registered deerhounds, which began in 1954 on Dava Moor, further north in the Scottish Highlands.

After the formalities were complete and we had heard a swift but informative lecture on the basics of hare coursing and tips for humanely dispatching a hare when caught, a line of spectators was formed. Flag steward and pickers-up took their positions and we were on our way, treading slowly and stealthily through the coarse, tangled heather.

The bitch I had entered was drawn last in the main stake of the event. Although I had a long wait to see how she fared in her first organised outing, there was an abundance of exciting courses to watch to pass the time.

To some people, six years may seem too old for a deer-hound to be dropped into organised hare coursing; indeed, some examples of the breed never reach this age, never mind carry on working past it. But Gwen was fit and a proven taker of hares in daylight and with the aid of a lamp at night. I doubt if there were many pure-bred deerhounds living in Great Britain at that time that could account for more hares than this versatile bitch!

I have a theory that the less intelligent a running dog, the better it is at coursing. Let me explain. A dog with the brains to follow the windings of a fleeing hare will catch rather than course. Running cunning is penalised in the organised hare coursing world. Instead, the main objective on the coursing plane is not to kill, but to accumulate points which are awarded to dogs for making the hare work, for turns, twists, jinks and so on.

From the day she nervously arrived on a ferry from Northern Ireland, I had helped in the rearing of this deerhound and was involved in every aspect of Gwen's training. I knew well her prowess as a taker of hares, but as a collector of points I knew nothing about her and could not estimate how she would perform.

The Duke of Norfolk drew up the first acknowledged rules for coursing for Queen Elizabeth I, and although killing hares has never been the true aim of coursing since the National Coursing Club took control of the sport in 1858, from time to time deerhounds do kill hares during a chase. The judge, Mr Mosey, is one of the top men in his field and during discussion the night before, over a delicious meal of Aberdeen Angus steak, he told us he rarely awards points for a kill.

The heather grabbed at our feet as we moved over the moor and hares soon began to lift from their forms, exploding from the ground like white cannon-balls. Many of the deerhounds slipped in pairs coursed well and accounted for

A pair of deerhounds working the hare well

numerous kills. Darren, an experienced deerhound slipper and handler, attempted to compensate for this by giving the powerful running hounds longer slips. But still the dogs caught hare after hare as they sped with loping strides over heather and grass.

In some running situations, the Scottish deerhound's physical size can hamper its hunting ability to a small degree, but here on its home ground the dog is at least equal to any of its contemporaries or mongrel relations.

I believe one of the main factors in this weekend's large haul of hares was the number of quality workers and fewer of the more cumbersome show-orientated animals being entered. There are show deerhounds that can run well, but in most cases the latter are pets that have lost their natural desire to chase and are only there to make up the numbers or at the whim of their owners. On the testing coursing stage, a dog wins on merit as there are no strings for owners to pull on the moors. Another factor was the number of hares, which I have noticed tend to be easier to catch when found in large quantities. A solitary hare or small pocket of hares is always difficult to take and that much more of a test for any dog.

On this particular occasion, the chases varied from those where the back-ends of hounds disappeared out of sight over a hillock, to those where you could see every twist and turn with the dogs almost within touching distance of their prey. But eventually, after a good cross section of courses, it was the turn of our bitch.

Our old girl was matched against one of her younger nephews, Rosslyn Hamish, a much larger dog, but this didn't detract from the fact that he had well-established coursing credentials and had a formidable working ancestry. His sire was Killoeter Lachie, a large, male deerhound that always surprised and entertained, as he was able to get down to the most awkward of hares, and his stamina and determination meant he was always one of the last hounds running at the

The deerhound with the white collar doing all the work

31

end of the day. His dam was the famous champion, Rosslyn Carrick.

The advancing line of spectators soon lifted a large, white-coated hare from the heather. Darren did well to hold on to the two eager dogs. He stumbled and strained to allow the hare as long a head start as possible before releasing them. Because of the undulating ground, Gwen must have been slightly unsighted from the slip, which gave Hamish a slender, early advantage.

During the long run up, where a good number of points can be won or lost, Gwen was running more or less to catch up with Hamish, but eventually she spotted the fleeing hare and turned on the power, but the gap was too great for her to make up and her opponent got to the hare first. He turned the beast sharply to his left. Gwen saw an opportunity and ran to cut the creature off at the pass, then, doing what years of hunting experience had taught her, she threw herself forward to take the hare with a quick strike, her strong jaws clamping vice-like across the creature's back. The hare was hers. Many hours of retrieving training were rewarded as she returned her catch to my outstretched hand, while fighting off Hamish who clearly believed he had done enough to claim the spoils – Gwen was having none of it.

I had travelled over 100 miles from home and home comforts to enter this competition, but Gwen's first competitive run had ended after just 20 seconds. She killed the hare but lost the course. It is a great pity points were not awarded for striking ability. If they were it might have helped her progress into the next round instead of being relegated to the first round losers' stake.

During the first day, as the calls of the grouse echoed from the hillsides, there were many courses for the gath-

Gwen retrieving the hare

ered enthusiasts to enjoy. The 'queen bee' of the deerhound-coursing world at that time, Coronach Luckpenny, together with Campsiefell Coire and a number of pups born of a well-planned union between Rohanis Firespur and Luck-penny, were all doing well.

The daylight hours at this time of the year are over in the blink of an eye, and as darkness fell the last remaining courses were completed, leaving only the semi-finals and fi-nals to be run the following day. As I drove from the moor, following the bright beams of vehicle headlights, the only sounds were the beating of my heart and the occasional pant or stretching yawn from a tired dog behind me, squeezed into a space into which even a diminutive whippet would have found it difficult to fit.

I awoke with excitement next morning as dawn was about to break. After a hearty, full Scottish breakfast, we travelled once more to our hunting destination, a procession of cars and four-wheel-drive vehicles snaking along roads that rarely saw so much traffic on a single day. On this second day, we were once again treated to some outstanding hare coursing.

Over both days of the competition I observed closely not only on my bitch, but also one particular male deerhound, Coronach Penny's Chieftain, which belonged to Sheila Sharp. I had already seen him taking major honours some weeks earlier on similar coursing grounds in Aberdeenshire. Although only 18 months old, he already possessed everything you could wish for in a good coursing deerhound: pace, stamina, good turning ability for his size, and that inborn desire to get to the hare that sets some dogs above the rest.

On one outstanding chase, which saw Sheila's dog disappear over a brow, then up a steep hill, this dog bumped and barged his way to the front before returning in no time at all, easily passing his opponent. The points were already won as he returned, still on the back of a hare. Roinneach (the kennel name of Sheila's dog), took out the hare right in front of the line, to my excited cries of 'Go on, my lad!'

After this gruelling chase, he went on to win the competition on a course that was worthy of any final, although the hare escaped to run another day and hopefully to raise young as strong as it was. This young hound was without doubt the finest, hare-coursing, male deerhound I had ever seen in action.

'Unfortunately he's got one major fault,' I said to my good friend, Jimmy Vickers, who was walking beside me at this point.

'A fault? And what is that?' Jimmy asked quietly from the corner of his mouth, at the same time bending towards me to conceal our surreptitious conversation.

'He doesn't belong to me,' I whispered. Jimmy roared

with laughter and strode off, head shaking, to pass on my comments to all and sundry.

With the competitive running now completed, a spot of social coursing took place. These chases saw a number of keen enthusiasts having a go at slipping and my bitch took another couple of hares on the way back. When finally we returned to our base, the presentation of trophies took place against the backdrop of the moors.

Now was the time to mull over the day's coursing and to relive some of the exciting talking points from the previous day. This was the end of the event and participants and spectators now set off home, some having to drive for many hours, others travelling by boat or plane back to the USA or Germany.

Once again, the hills had done their job, providing the Deerhound Club with enough hares for two days' sport. We in turn left a hare population slightly down in numbers, but all that much stronger because of it.

Our bitch Gwen was three weeks in pup on this occasion, so she would soon have to be laid up for well-earned maternity leave. Before her rest began she won her way through, against lurchers, to the semi-final of a lamping competition run by the Northumberland and Durham Working Lurcher Club, with rabbits the quarry on this occasion.

I will never forget my 1998 visits to Caledonia to observe the indigenous wildlife and to take part in that particular coursing event. It is not only the beauty of Scotland that makes it so different and more appealing compared to other locations. It is the feel and smell of the place, a charm that I believe cannot be found in any other country of the world.

I was so impressed by the ability of Sheila Sharp's winning dog I contacted her with a view to using him as a mate for

Gwen on the back of a hare

my young bitch Meg. She kindly agreed, and my father and I were the first in a line of breeders to use him as a stud. This union produced a wonderful litter of what I would deem typical Doherty deerhounds, as our smaller framed bitches can afford to be mated with dogs of substance without fear that the resulting progeny will be too big or coarse, or outside the breed standard.

Coronach Penny's Chieftain, as I had always predicted, became one of the all-time coursing greats. He was unbeaten for many seasons in organised competition. The first hound to defeat him was one of his own progeny, bred by us: Doxhope Lady Gwendolyn. Her dam was Doxhope Lady Annadaille.

CHAPTER 3

SAND, GRIT AND DETERMINATION

I began the 1996 season of hunting rabbits with dogs with a mission to reach new sporting heights for me and my pack, mainly through the activity of lamping.

I regularly took part – successfully – in the nocturnal hunting pursuit of lamping as a result of my long involvement with lurchers and my desire to test my dogs in all possible working situations. By dint of the nature of this hunting technique, which allows more prey to be found in one night than during many days, I consistently achieved large hauls and my reputation as a rabbit catcher secured much sought after permission to work my lurchers and deerhounds on many Northumberland and Scottish border farms.

My next jaunt in the darkness and shadows, however, was as a result of permission on well-laden hunting lands acquired by an old hunting and family friend, John (Ginger) Alderton from the Northumberland mining town of Ashington. Les White, a noted hunter from the seaport of Blyth and a regular contributor to various sporting magazines, once described Ashington as 'the lurcher capital of England', and Ginger regularly boasted of being 'the oldest poacher in town'.

The area around this mid-Northumberland location certainly always possessed more than its fair share of running dogs: proper lurchers, strong looking curs which had long since replaced the whippets depicted in those Andy Cap cartoons. Ginger was indeed around when I moved

Gwen (Rosslyn Fling)

from the neighbouring mining town of Bedlington in the early 70s. His hard-earned reputation of being a man o' the fields was built around him always possessing good hunting dogs.

John came from the village of Newbiggin-by-the-Sea, where men are hard-bitten and tough. A collection of facial scars and less than a full complement of teeth were common in this tough place as the by-products of arguments about leeks, pigeons, trotting horses and lurchers. Dogs in many situations were high in the pecking order, treated sometimes even more highly than family members. I have witnessed small children standing on cold, linoleum-covered floors shivering, as an injured dog, stitched or still wet after a healing wash of Epsom salts and water, replaced them in their warm beds.

Through working running dogs for many decades, Ginger had, like me, secured permission from many farmers to follow his particular hunting hobbies over their land. While my land was secured mainly because of my vermin controlling activities, Ginger obtained permission because of his talent for horse breaking, or as reward for being temporarily employed as a hard-working farm hand during the sweating, back-breaking harvesting season.

The land picked for this particular night out was situated less than a mile from the steel-grey waters of the North Sea. To the north of the farm stands Bamburgh Castle, one of the finest landmarks on the north-east coast, perched high on a basalt outcrop. The craggy ruins of Dunstanburgh castle dominate a lonely stretch of coast to the south. This part of Northumberland has always been noted as a productive area for game.

The verdure of Ginger's farm stretches towards the sea where it meets wide strips of sallow sand dunes. The dunes are dressed with marram, sea lyme and sea couch grasses and belong to what was then the National Trust.

The dunes provide summer nesting environments for various waders and sea birds. Redshanks, ringed plovers and eider ducks all make their well-camouflaged homes on the ground amid viper's bugloss, lesser ragwort and hound's tongue. The area also plays temporary host to visiting sand martins that enjoy our shores during the warm, midge-filled summer months. These welcome guests nest in deep holes burrowed horizontally into the steeper, sandy bank sides. During the replenishing seasons, I have spent many peaceful evenings observing the high-speed antics of these nimble birds, listening to their chitter-chatter as they skim past me with masterful precision.

The sandy embankments are also ideal environments for

rabbits to burrow. The well-established warrens here are exceptionally deep due to the ease with which they can be excavated. In the past, I have worked this area using ferrets and nets, but the thundering noise synonymous with a bolting rabbit is rarely heard, masked by the unusual depth of these burrows. In my view, these rabbit residences have never reached their full potential as productive ferreting grounds.

The entire dunes are strewn with such warrens and although ensuring a copious amount of rabbits, it is awkward and treacherous terrain. My lamping friends and I had worked these dunes, and other such ground, many times over the years, so we were aware of all the hidden dangers and natural pitfalls that lurked in the shadows.

It was early evening when our lamping team of Ginger, George Smith (Big Pie) and I set off for the beckoning hunting grounds. At over 20 stones in weight, George re-

Deerhounds and lurcher scanning the grassy dunes

ally tested the suspension of the aging vehicle in which we travelled. My companions both took deerhound-blooded lurchers on this jaunt. My eldest, pure-bred deerhound bitch, Gwen, accompanied me. I could have, and usually would have, taken along one of my lurchers, these being more suited to this ground and its awkwardness, but I do like to keep my deerhounds fit and active as well as familiarise them with as many different hunting forms and conditions as possible.

Once settled, George, a lurcherman of immense experience and another born-and-bred product of Newbiggin, launched into telling tales and anecdotes of poaching exploits and illicit hunting expeditions from his past. Some people connected with lurcherdom don't have what it takes to remember events of long ago and dogs gone by. This man can tell the history and background of almost every local running dog, who bred and owned them, what quarry they were famous for taking and, in some instances, individual performances. He really has a most phenomenal memory, and I sat in awe taking in all he had to tell.

By the time we arrived at our hunting destination, the westerly wind that had blown so angrily during the day had subsided to a breeze, and the dark sky was quickly filling with clouds; these swallowed up the moon, leaving the heavens murky which was not the ideal black-as-coal situation, but good enough for lamping nevertheless. Out at sea, the orange glow of ships anchored for the night flickered in the darkness, while inshore the cries of the farmer's peacocks echoed eerily.

The night's sport started slowly but, as we ventured further into the dunes, we picked up rabbits at regular intervals, taking turns to slip our dogs one at a time. We never allowed more than one dog to chase in the darkness as this could easily be a recipe for disaster.

Lamping for rabbits on the undulating dunes requires a different game plan than working on flatter, more sparsely-covered terrain. In particular, the lamp must be kept illuminated for longer periods. The most effective method for me is to allow my dog to walk free, trotting contently at my heels. I then shine the lamp over every inch of the dunes and grass, letting the 250,000 candle-power beam do its work of probing every shadow. Seeing a rabbit spurs the dog into action and sometimes I have to run to ensure that dog and quarry are kept within the beam. This method can only be implemented efficiently if the dog is rock steady and totally biddable, traits my well-trained lurchers and intelligent deerhounds possess in abundance. With individual lampers less than 50 yards apart at times, an unruly dog could spoil an evening's sport, running between lamps sending all the nervous rabbits in the vicinity to ground.

Eventually we came to a place where the natural contours of the dunes meant we could separate. Big Pie took the left flank which bordered on to the lapping water's edge, Ginger scanned the middle sector and I was positioned on the right boundary, which continually changed from fence to dry-stone wall then back again.

As I worked my section, I occasionally stopped to observe the pencil-like beams from my two friends' lamps swishing across the dunes like flashes of lightning. Then I continued along the path created by generations of stock, ramblers and other visitors to this spot, my lamp lighting the way as I attempted to pinpoint something for Gwen to chase.

Suddenly, I caught a rabbit in the beam, sitting feeding

quite unperturbed next to the weather-beaten wall. I ran awkwardly towards it, calling for Gwen who was following closely. As soon as the dog spotted the creature she shot past me as I dodged through the thicker grass. I held the lamp above my head, pointing the beam towards the wall as I temporarily lost sight of our quarry. Then, as my line of sight was restored, the rabbit, startled by our clumsy intrusion, made off at speed. My bitch quickly homed in on it as it turned and jinked this way and that like an agile hare. I kept the spot of light fixed on the creature as it ran for sanctuary in the longer grass away from the wall. Gwen followed and I watched as she got closer and closer. I saw her head go down among the shadows, emerging moments later with the squealing rabbit locked tightly in her jaws. She loped back towards me through the long grass with her prey bouncing in her mouth. When she placed it in my waiting hand, I quickly dispatched it. The next three chases resembled this first one, with most rabbits being caught in the longer grass.

From my position close to the wall, I saw a fair number of rabbits, as I expected, making their way back towards this barrier in a last ditch attempt to avoid the pursuing dog. This helped me secure a decent tally with Gwen on the night. The solid barrier of a wall is always helpful when lamping, unlike for example an unfenced plantation edge. The well-known trick of the trade of allowing the rabbit to run at speed towards the wall then, at the last moment, switching the light off for a split second, is a ploy I used to good effect. It causes the creature to turn from the wall into the darkness, sometimes straight into the dog's mouth. I have also seen other night-time hunters shaking the light vigorously. This too causes the rabbit to become disorientated and more likely to make mistakes but tends to make me dizzy so I never employ it. It's best to stick to what you are comfortable with.

Apart from rabbits, my deerhound bitch also obtained the course of a solitary hare, which mistakenly ventured into the beam. As a rule we don't often race these wonderful creatures on the lamp at this location, as stocks are only just building up again after shooting and poaching took their toll at a time before Ginger was enrolled to help police it.

Gwen is a proven hare killer and has taken a fair number in her lifetime. However this leggy hare possessed more than the usual amount of strength, agility and cunning and completely outwitted my old girl. It left her following a trail of scent through the long grass towards what looked like a hole in the fence that had been used as an escape route on more than one occasion.

Further on, Gwen also chased an old dog fox, whose musky smell drifting heavily on the breeze helped give him away. A long slip was a distance she never really made up before the creature stole through a bracken-covered gap in the fence and away to safety.

All my deerhounds have a natural hatred of foxes and Gwen is no exception. She can easily outrun a fox given fair law and possessed more than enough strength to bowl over and make fairly easy work of dispatching a prey that bites back.

The discipline that Ginger, Big Pie and I needed to keep our positions had vanished during the excitement of numerous chases. At one point, I exchanged places with Ginger as he chased after his dog towards the ancient wall and I stalked a rabbit into the depths of the long grass where my companion would have been. Teamwork is essential, and we quickly swapped back to our original places.

After a while, we all emerged from our chases and met up quite near our pre-determined finishing point, a place where the land once again narrowed and pointed out towards the sea. A line of cottages lay to our right and inquisitive faces peeped out from behind thick curtains.

Ginger and Pie had both done well with their dogs. My deerhound, suited physically to this rougher terrain, almost attained the maximum chase to kill ratio, and was only two rabbits behind the lurchers in her final tally.

For some running dog enthusiasts, chasing rabbits on sand dunes conjures up all types of unsavoury associations. Indeed, many lurchermen I know never allow their dogs to work this most difficult test, possibly with some justification, as many dogs have been injured or even killed running there. However, intelligent dogs will quickly learn how to run safely on the dunes and, although a testing ground, it can also be quite a productive place where large numbers of rabbits can be taken.

After a brief rest and review of our dogs' performances, we set off once again. Although the plan was to take turns, the enthusiastic Ginger slipped his dog on everything that remotely resembled a rabbit: grass sods, rocks and even ground-roosting birds were not spared.

So far that night the dunes had been somewhat tame, but as we slowly made our way back towards the farm, picking up a few straggler rabbits on the way, they finally lived up to their reputation. Not for our dogs, however, but for the 'oldest poacher in town'. At one point, the only clues to the whereabouts of the elder statesman of our group were his muffled cries and a fawn, broken-haired lurcher marking the hole that had engulfed his master. George and I both burst into uncontrollable bouts of laughter, as Pie's giant, shovel-like hands pulled Ginger out from the ground with ease.

At the end of our evening foray we packed our haul, settled the dogs and left the freshness of the coast satisfied hunters with tired but fitter canine companions. How we got everything into that Austin Metro was a miracle to say the least.

This was another hunt to add to my many exciting memories of a successful lamping season. Three days later, the same hound which ran rabbits in such a determined, workman-like fashion that cold evening, won fourth place in a very strong, postgraduate class at the Scottish Kennel Club Championship Show in Edinburgh. This demonstrates the versatility of the Scottish deerhound, able to work in hostile environments then exhibit a few days later in less treacherous situations.

CHAPTER 4

HOSTILE SCOTTISH HILLS

As the dog and I walked our usual haunts, where the bare branches reminded us of how close we were to winter, I said to her, 'Meg, we will soon be treading across ancient moors, a place where there are so many hares, you will crave to run riot.'

The bright bitch sensed the excitement in my tone of voice and responded by shoving herself affectionately against my leg, a paw raised from the ground, her long tail waving like a conductor's baton shaping the music of a large orchestra. 'In other words,' I said, 'we are off to bonny Scotland.'

I had recently been invited by a friend for a day's coursing of blue hares over the Scottish borders. As a grade 'A' hunter-gatherer, I accepted with alacrity. My kilt-clad host for the day was a poacher turned gamekeeper turned poacher – a weird situation and difficult to explain. Jock lived in a tied cottage and was practically self-sufficient. His home on the estate was secured on the understanding that he would act on the landowner's whims, which in effect gave him a roof over his head but brought in no income. This he got from an assortment of activities, some legal and others a tad more illicit.

My first encounter with Jock was at a lurcher show on the Duke of Buccleuch's land. He was a countryman like me, interested in wildlife, and he was as brilliant with all dogs as he was obnoxious to most people. Every deerhound, lurcher and terrier I ever took to his place saw him as a god and in-stantly worshipped him.

His domain was very similar to the Scottish, game-abundant locations I had attended many times over the years on organised coursing events. So I was fully aware of what to expect physically: all the symptoms of a tiring walk in the desert, but with crisp heather instead of sinking sand and a constant, chilling wind rather than humid heat.

This border terrain, where the air is fresh and the scenery most alluring, possesses its own impressive and beguiling charm. But the one time gateway of William Wallace for his plundering raids into Northumberland and along the Tyne valley is more often than not spoken of in reverential rather than affectionate tones. Anyone who has

The author with a leash of hunting deerhounds

hunted this wild land, or tramped the moors beating at a grouse shoot, will know exactly what is meant. Whether the hunter is coursing hares in the very heart of the hills or lamping around its rabbit infested fringes, this is arduous country. Because of this, both dogs and owners need to be fit and in good physical condition.

My leash of deerhounds, Gwen, Meg and Becky, were all primed and ready for the day out. Mother and daughters were exercised to peak fitness through a regime that included many outings catching rabbits on the lamp, daylight work on the same quarry in conjunction with ferrets and of course, the occasional chase of a supercharged hare, a cunning fox or a powerful, running deer. All three hounds had begun their organised, hare coursing careers over the last few seasons, but on this excursion there was not going to be the same law afforded to such staged hunting events.

My Scottish mate couldn't see the point of these competitions. He possessed a 'must be caught' attitude to anything classed as game and together we had prepared quite a different game plan for this less formal jaunt, which was a day to take hares, not to course them.

Our idea was to advance with a deerhound each. The third hound would be allowed to walk free, getting the feel of the place. The unleashed dog would assist us in seeking out hares hiding beneath the heather and course any that it put up or were lifted by our smaller than usual line. This alternating of the dogs would spread the workload but, if required on an exceptionally strong hare, a second dog could be released. At no time though would all three hounds be off the lead together on a chase. We believed this method would prove effective, securing us plenty of courses and ample hares to carry back at the end of the day.

Dogs from good, working strains of deerhound unsullied by show trends, and most lurcher composites, are quite capable of taking blue hares consistently without the assistance of another dog. Any running dog of average ability will always catch a good percentage of what they chase and good dogs should rarely miss.

At the time of my visit, the estate's gamekeepers had begun shooting these fascinating creatures as part of an annual cull. Their method was to use .22 long-rifles at night, with a lamp shone from their four-wheel drive vehicles. This is a very efficient form of control for both hares and rabbits, and I can remember on a previous visit to one keeper seeing the back of his Toyota Hi-Lux filled level with blues hares. It was still fairly early in the hunting season, but already a fair amount of the estate's annual cull tally of 700 hares had been accounted for. What a great pity. I am a great believer that hares were designed to run, and therefore only to be chased, never shot or snared. It seems to me that shooting or snaring is an insult to these creatures, but the estate has to function and be profitable. This estate has protected hares for many decades, so they obviously know what they are talking about, at least in the way of conserving stocks.

Our base for the visit was a weary-looking cottage and we travelled from there to our destination in an old, very noisy, short-wheel-based Landrover that probably possessed a maintenance record of epic proportions. We bounced leap-frog style along a rising track, all the while trying not to regurgitate our breakfast stovies. We were aiming for higher ground where every crease and fold of the landscape was flecked white with snow. This area, well above sea-level, is always expected to hold a good number of blue hares, and we had certainly seen many on the move on our trek up the hillside. Once parked, and with the noise of the four-wheel drive's engine still ringing in our ears, we set off on foot.

The endless sea of heather which lay in front of us was richly tinted with autumnal colours and drew our eyes towards the remote, steel-grey horizon. Gwen began as the free hound, skipping over the coarse heather carpet until she picked up the scent left by a travelling hare. Suddenly, from the warmth and seclusion of its shallow seat, the hare lifted. The first chase of the morning was on.

When hares lift in dense heather like this, they scan the ground for shorter, cropped or burnt off heather

Gwen closing in on her hare

where they can make better speed. They don't have the luxury of gates, hedges or fences as pre-planned escape routes like their brown cousins and remaining too long in the denser, longer heather gives an advantage to the pursing deerhound with its loping running style. This particular hare did make it to the short stuff, but not before the hound made up a lot of ground on her.

Once the hare was on more favourable territory, an epic course ensued with many turns and twists before my hound struck and secured her prey. One excellent course and one strong hare caught – not a bad beginning to our morning's sport, and testimony to our preparation of a plan that was to work well time after time.

At this time of year, these plucky, blue hares are beginning to change colour and some are already dressed in a cloak of ermine. They are not clones however, and there can be much variation in pigment between individuals, some mottled with light brown, others with grey. There have been various suggestions as to how this colour change occurs. It was once thought it was caused by a complete moult. Later, more scientific, theories imply it is more due to sensors in the root of the hair which cause the pigment to alter at low temperatures.

Next, it was the turn of my particular baby, Meg, to walk without the leather slip lead. This bitch is the best quality hound that we kept back. She is actually faster than her mother, Gwen, and as a worker she too has taken every legitimate English quarry. Meg hunts by day and also by night. She jumps like a gazelle and retrieves to hand everything she catches. Meg possesses a nose, but like the majority of the breed she just hasn't realised she can use it to find interesting things to chase.

During Meg's first turn as the unrestrained dog, a rangy hare did lift in front of her, put up more because of being nervous than by any useful scenting ability of my dog. This hare also made for one of the many strips of short heather that border the coarser patches of vegetation like a decorative frame. A slightly longer course resulted, again with many twists and a couple of good turns by the pair. Over rough, undulating ground they went but eventually, the result was the same as Gwen's run, though lacking her fierce strike and ending instead in a more controlled stoop and picking-up. This hare was also carried back to the group. What a godsend it is to have dogs that retrieve well! I rewarded my bitch's success with verbal praise and she seemed to know that I was more than pleased.

Jock's steady hands fastened Meg securely in a slip-lead and then he released her sister Becky, allowing her the privilege of roaming free. If Meg was my particular favourite, a teacher's pet, then without doubt Becky was my Dad's darling. He really doted on this bitch, and she in turn gave him hours of pleasure when they journeyed the local fields together. I remember him proudly telling me about one day when Becky was off the lead, rummaging in the undergrowth. She returned carrying a white, plastic shopping bag, her tail swinging like a pendulum. Dad took the carrier from her, folded it, and put it in his inside pocket. A while later, Becky was off in hot pursuit of a rabbit among the thick briars. She caught her prey and presented it into my Dad's hand. He duly took out the bag and placed the rabbit inside. He always swore she brought him that bag because she knew she was going to get a rabbit for him that day and he would require something in which to carry it.

As litter siblings, Meg and Becky showed very few genetic similarities. Both were keen workers but this is where any likeness ended. As a pup, Meg was as long as a crocodile, while her sister was more short-coupled. Meg, even at an early age, oozed quality. At the same age, Becky showed nothing and was moved on, only to be bought back at a later age. At this point in the evolution of Doxhope kennels, Becky was probably our finest working hound. She was definitely the fastest and most agile, and her scenting ability was the best I had witnessed in any pure-bred, Scottish deerhound, from any kennel.

Immediately Becky's busy nose began to investigate the wiry ground. The rest of us watched her affectionately, with

Becky coursing her first hare of the day

only an occasional glance at the broader landscape in case a cunning hare was attempting to avoid us. Her scenting ability, a trait I knew so well, was also familiar to Jock and all my dogs.

At last she caught a scent. She sniffed and sniffed again, her pace quickening while her tail began to wag furiously.

'She's on to one,' I called out to Jock as Becky began to accelerate and the deerhounds at our sides reared up excitedly.

Suddenly, a hare that had been lying motionless lifted from its form a few yards in front of the dog. Its long ears were pinned flat to its back, its eyes wild as it took flight. The lift was short, and it took only a few seconds before Becky matched the initial take-off speed of the hare.

Twist for twist and turn for turn the bitch matched her tricky opponent. This was a strong, agile hare, one that could so easily have been shot had the visiting gamekeepers spotted her with their million candle-powered lamps. But against a running dog, at least it stood a sporting chance.

The beginning of the chase had seen the pair going away from us. Now the hare was turned and both dog and beast were heading back. As they veered broadside on, the snapping jaws of the dog could be clearly heard. The tethered deerhounds whined their encouragement. A series of quick jinks then a final, life-taking lunge and the hare was Becky's. Three hares chased, three hares caught, a ratio that couldn't be bettered.

By lunchtime our team was lucky enough to have obtained nearly a dozen good courses, catching no less than eight hares. To allow the dogs a well-earned break, we decided to have a rest. Well, we may have said it was for the well-being of our canine chums, but in reality it was more for our benefit. Walking on heather is a very energy-sapping pastime indeed. We fashioned a comfortable settee on the ground, sinking into a mound of amber grass to ponder our morning's sport and admire the fantastic scenery. It is so beautiful and tranquil in these border hills.

'Don't you just love the sounds of nature?' I asked Jock, as he relaxed.

Jock's head slowly turned, 'Yes, listen to its talk. But pay attention to the silences too, for there is just as much in what's not said, as in what is.' Indeed, learning to think like this man remains a skill I have yet to develop fully.

Resting there, time and space was temporarily forgotten as my mind wandered dreamily into the past. Curlews circled high above us with their haunting cries. Looking towards a stream, I watched a dipper's rock-hopping quest for its dinner as it plunged repeatedly into the icy waters and ran, submerged, over the gravelled river bed. A solitary tail-dipping, ring ouzel and a small flock of twites, or mountain linnets as my Scottish friend calls them, were among the other points of ornithological interest.

Suddenly, I was awakened from my daydreams by a wet, sticky tongue completely engulfing my ear. This was the bell to signify our dinner break was over. Any Scottish deerhound owner will know what I mean when I speak of this form of greeting. These gentle giants either welcome you in this way, or with an uncomfortable nudge to the 'nether regions'. The latter can be most embarrassing, as it frequently occurs when chatting in mixed company or when waiting your turn in the show ring at a championship show.

We vacated our seats and left the haul of hares lying belly-up where they could be easily retrieved after our shift, which still had a few more hours to go. We set off once more with the hounds raring for further sport, rejuvenated by their rest.

The stamina of a fit, working deerhound is quite incredible, especially considering how much effort it puts into its running style. Archibald McNeill, one of the gentlemen responsible for the revival of the hound during the 1800s in what is sometimes referred to as the 'Colonsay period', was reported to have written, 'It is difficult to imagine how any race of dog could ever again be produced possessing such a combination of qualities as the Scottish deerhound.' Seeing good examples of these working dogs running at full tilt over lavender-dressed hills is truly one of the finest sights I have ever witnessed.

This picturesque, typically Scottish, scene of which we were so fortunate to be a part also has a darker, more sinister side in the form of hidden drainage ditches and natural holes and trenches scattered across the moor. These are partly concealed by heather, forming traps for the unsuspecting, and over the seasons I have seen hounds take some horrendous tumbles. Deerhounds, by virtue of their size, usually take falls badly. To date, I have had no fatalities and, surprisingly, no bad injuries partly because of the soundness of my stock and partly out of sheer good luck.

Injuries to dew claws are among the most common. I always remove dew claws from my lurcher pups at around three or four days of age, but they remain on all my working deerhounds. I am truly amazed at the low frequency of injuries to this redundant extremity. I have seen lurchers with dew claws sustain some horrible cuts as the curved nail is pulled back or fouled on a rock or sharp stone.

Some would say, 'Yes, but the deerhound doesn't turn like a lurcher when chasing' – but I can assure these folk that good working deerhounds put an immense amount of physical effort into whatever they are chasing.

The first kill of the day's second half went to Becky. What a wonderful bitch she is. Her running style is like that of a good lurcher, her light frame allows a nimbleness not usually found in the modern Celtic hound, and she has speed to burn. She is the type of bitch that you always feel is going to catch her prey when slipped.

This hare lifted a fair distance from us, a space far in excess of what we were accustomed to that day, in fact, longer than any slip I had witnessed at organised coursing events. Becky glided over the moor and quickly got to the hare and bent the creature to the left. As the pair raced in front of us, we were able to see the bitch's ability to make the hare work. Through a letch† they dipped, sending a fountain of red grouse skyward as the pair gatecrashed the family gathering. Both dog and hare were now making towards us at a fair old rate of knots and it was time to take a firmer hold of the other two dogs in our possession. Closer and closer they came and Meg and Gwen danced and reared. Jock and I did our best to hold the eager animals at the same time as keeping our eyes on Becky and the hare. The whites of their eyes could almost be seen when Becky dipped to pick up the hare. Then the brakes went on and she stopped just in front of us. I handed my dog to Jock and sorted out Becky and her new kicking and threshing possession.

That done we once again strode on, this time with Meg

†ravine, gully

working free. On her hare she ran with cunning, cutting the hare off on numerous occasions. Even though she was mimicking her sister Becky's running style, the hare escaped and survived to run again another day.

The next hare however didn't have the same skill or good fortune. Gwen once again kept up her excellent record of taking out a fair percentage of the blue hares she chased.

Injury free, we had reached a point on our expedition where we would have to turn back. Another 14 courses had been obtained between the three hounds during the cold but sunny afternoon, eight of these chases being successful. The final tally was now 16 hares; not the best I had achieved on similar outings but respectable nevertheless. The ones that got away? Well, these could be categorised as the strongest which survived, hopefully to breed in the future – if they dodged the keeper's bullets over the next few weeks, that is!

The last two courses of the day were extremely lengthy affairs and did seem to take a lot out of the dogs that ran them. This helped us in making the decision the day was over. True dog men should always be aware of when their wards have had enough. It is all too easy to get caught up in the feverish activity of coursing hares or lamping rabbits. This is when the dog's health and well being can be temporarily forgotten. I have unfortunately witnessed dogs collapse because of too much work over too short a space of time. I have helped to carry dogs that were exhausted and completely incapacitated. I have also helped to bury one or two. Not a pretty sight or an experience I like to take part in.

Because the hills cover a huge area, we hadn't realised

Bill, Becky and a number of mountain hares

how great a distance we had travelled from the spot where we had left our morning's spoils. Carrying all those hares back, I felt as if I had died and gone to heaven. At one point I fell to my knees totally exhausted, much to the amusement of my younger and so much fitter friend.

Altogether, the day was a great experience and I thoroughly enjoyed seeing the deerhounds performing on the history-steeped Lammermuirs, the backbone of Scotland's Lothian Region. I had few reservations about the day, but the main one was, 'I wish there was an easier way to navigate those bloody hills.'

CHAPTER 5
DEERHOUNDS, LURCHERS AND FERRETS

My enthusiastic involvement in hunting and my avid inter-est in all living creatures have always played a major part in my life. During my long attachment to running dogs, and in particular using them for taking rabbits, I have never been the type of person to shirk an opportunity to get my dogs out into the fields, or to restrict them from participating in activities wrongly deemed by others as unsuitable.

I say wrongly because, as in all hobbies and walks of life, there are people all too eager to over-ice any cake they are attempt-ing to bake. From experience, those who deride certain breeds or crosses have rarely owned or worked an example of the dog and are usually novices or ill informed.

As a dog man of long-standing, my career has been both illus-trious and interesting. Every serious keeper of dogs should have a goal, and I am no exception. My objective has always been to attain as high a level of success as possible with my lurchers and later with my deerhounds, taking them into all the hunting dis-ciplines that I favour.

My lurchers were purposely bred to be good all-rounders, but individual dogs in my pack have become quite specialist in vari-ous fields of work. Some excel on daylight work catching hare and rabbit, others shine in the nocturnal sport of lamping, but in the main they are jacks of all trades, adapting readily to anything I throw at them.

My pure-bred deerhounds, although never possessing the abil-ity to match the sheer versatility of their cross-bred relations, have also achieved a certain degree of all-round hunting success.

The Scottish deerhound was primarily developed to do what it says on the tin: to hunt deer. It has been illegal to take deer with dogs in Scotland since 1959, but even prior to the 2004 Hunting Act in England and Wales, which forbids such activities, horned adversaries of any type would hardly ever have been classed as a main sporting quarry by any modern-day deerhound owner.

This antiquated sport of lairds, chieftains, kings and queens, slowly over the centuries, was forced into redundancy by the 'ban this, ban that' attitude of legislators. Deer have been supplanted by quarry species such as fox and hare by hunters keen to keep deerhounds a fit and working breed. But, alas, city politicians and others attempting to make names for themselves have also removed these creatures from the list of animals to chase. Now in 2006, we hunters are left with only the humble rabbit.

The rabbit, often depicted by fools as being easy to catch and thus not worthy of hunting, can be a testing quarry for the pure-bred deerhound in certain circumstances, mainly due to the creature's agility and a high take-off speed. One situation is when the nocturnal hunter is out to bag large numbers of this crop-destroying pest. At night, most dogs of any breed or type noted for their running prowess will make catching a rabbit or two look pretty straightforward. But how will the same animal fare when chasing 20, 40, 60 or even more on a cold night's work over inhospitable ground?

Another test that can prove to be awkward for some working deerhounds is ferreting, that is the dog working in daylight in conjunction with hard-grafting ferrets.

As with any specialist hunting, dogs particularly well suited to that type of challenge will evolve with the help of selective breeding. The sport of ferreting therefore has helped produce dogs with the attributes required to work efficiently with mustalid companions. Successful ferreting dogs are usually smaller composites, nimble and fleet of foot, although this has been proved many times not to be a finite list of requirements. The old-fashioned whippet or 'dyke backer' as they were often called in the North East of England, has since been replaced by diminutive lurchers, Bedlington terrier crosses being among a long list of favourites for many ferreting enthusiasts.

With smaller dogs so often stereotyped for ferreting work, you can imagine the look of complete disbelief on the landowner's face, when my deerhound bitch jumped out of the Diahatsu Fourtrak one day on a winter ferreting outing.

'This I will have to see to believe,' muttered the farmer, feeling the loins of my bitch. 'You'll have a job lifting this un over the fences, never mind catching a rabbit with it. Can she jump?'

I smiled and answered, 'Oh yes, she can jump.'

'A fiver if she catches more than one,' he wagered.

'Done,' I replied quickly, before he had any opportunity whatsoever to renege on the bet.

Now, this was hardly a gamble akin to that of Sir William St Clair and Robert the Bruce. It is said that Sir William wagered his own head on the success of his brace of deerhounds, Help and Hold, against a red deer in the Pentland Hills. Sir William bet his life against the lands on which the dogs were running and on the success of his pair. The deerhounds caught the deer in the middle of a burn and dragged it to the shore. Sir William won his gamble, but would I be as successful? Granted the stakes were not so high, but it was a wager nevertheless.

The rabbit-populated land we were working lies between Newcastle upon Tyne and the ancient village of Otterburn, near the Scottish border. This rough-grazing terrain is part of the Ray Estates owned by Viscount Davenport. The land epitomises how conservation and sporting interests can go hand in hand, where spectacular scenery houses a wealth of nature's treasures, testimony to the efforts and ideals of the conservation-minded landowner.

Dogs, ferrets and our hunting paraphernalia where all loaded

A working deerhound should be able to jump

into the long-wheel-based Land Rover and the farmer, game-keeper's son and I chugged across uneven fields and marshy fells heavily marked with tell-tale signs of coney. Rabbits, edgy and sensing danger, stood on their hind legs, watching us curiously with noses twitching. They munched as they observed our party, stooping from time to time for another mouthful of lush grass before lifting again to follow our progress. We rummaged around looking for warrens that were suitable and obviously occupied.

Once we found them, our initial plan was to cover all entrances and bolt holes with specially designed nets called purse nets. A ferret is then placed into one of the holes and disappears to work through the many tunnels and chambers in search of rabbits. The inhabitants are panicked by the noise and smell of the weasel-like creature hunting them. In an attempt to escape they bolt out of the holes and get caught in the net. In this situation, a dog is useful when rabbits, for various reasons, escape the clutches of the 2¼ inch mesh hemp nets, or when nets are intentionally not fitted and rabbits are allowed to escape for a dog to chase.

Ferreting on this occasion was not to be the net-covering-every-hole-type operation. We were seeking to secure a number of rabbits obviously, but we also hoped for some sport.

Although experience would never allow me to be so arrogant as to declare all ferreted rabbits straightforward to catch, this hunting discipline is fairly easy for most running dogs to come to terms with. They will usually learn quickly what is expected of them and in the right locations good results can be expected.

This country, although mainly soft, rolling grass fields circum-navigated by lichen-covered dry-stone walls, is strewn with what we in Northumberland call 'dyke castings', exposed mounds of earth stretching like giant, surface mole-runs across the entire length of fields in which they are situated. These convex, metre-high castings, now completely covered with a carpet of grasses and moss, are home to many rabbits, which find their excavation easier than tunnelling through the undisturbed soil of the area.

My tried and tested, and most successful, approach to working these rabbits is to start at one end of the casting, then ferret bury by bury. Once completed, each set of holes are back filled with soil, a grass sod or a large stone. We then move on to the next set, which is usually only a short distance away. Some rabbits when bolted will make for open ground. However a large majority will,

Deerhound marking a hole

with great regularity, make for the previously filled-in holes. With the chasing dog close behind, the rabbit becomes another statistic for the record books, as it attempts to find an entrance that no longer exists. Even if the rabbit makes for open ground, a decent lurcher or good coursing-type deerhound akin to that accompanying me on such a hunt, should still have a good chance of a kill. By stacking the odds in our favour with tricks of the trade like this 'back filling', we can secure larger hauls of rabbits, and put a smile on the face of a farmer who has actually worked out what each resident rabbit consumes in the way of grass.

Ferreting for me is not just a question of finding work for my dogs and sport for myself. In most cases, I am doing a job for the landowner, keeping rabbit numbers down to an acceptable level. So, after a day in the fields, I must have something to show for my endeavours.

Although I had never tested my deerhound, Gwen, in hunting with ferrets using the back-filling method, I was confident of her ability to put up a decent show. All deerhounds are fairly intelligent, sometimes too intelligent for their own good, and every other example of this breed I had tried in the past had passed the test with flying colours.

As our work began, the first rabbit of the day was caught by the deerhound, demonstrating once again the effectiveness of back filling. After a profound drum-roll from the ground beneath us, a rabbit bolted from its dark home, running flat-out in the direction of the holes we had just blocked. My deerhound pursued her prey with her usual zest to an opening which in normal circumstances would have given the rabbit protection. After a sudden stop and a moment of indecision, the rabbit was in the grasp of the dog's powerful jaws. The lurcher too enjoyed herself on the day, achieving plenty of success. My old bitch, Yella, is primarily a night hunter and in her working career had caught vast numbers of coney. On this outing, she took rabbit after rabbit with her usual efficiency, whether they were running to be greeted by blocked holes or dashing away from their sets seeking sanctuary in the labyrinth of longer grass and scrub or in the cracks and crevices of neighbouring dry-stone walls.

The grand dame of my kennels took to this daylight hunting without difficulty when introduced to it for the first time a few years ago, as a good, all-round lurcher should. She took over 40 rabbits on her maiden trial of the sport and since then has accounted for over 500 daylight rabbits.

Gwen, although lacking the liveliness of her diminutive companion, ran fairly well on the rabbits making for open ground. Her lack of nimbleness was replaced by determination and striking ability – typical hunting characteristics of the deerhounds my father and I co-produced. This workman-like hound couldn't match Yella's chase-to-catch ratio, and I wouldn't have expected her to, but she missed very little on the day and gave a good overall account of herself.

On one chase, due to the fumbling fingers of the gamekeeper's son, she was slipped late but made up ground well. Gwen is a sensible dog so when her adversary began to turn she was able to respond quickly and, although not matching the rabbit's tight turns, she did enough to win the contest.

Gwen kick-started her daylight rabbit catching by securing a personal best of a dozen rabbits during that foray. This was surpassed by my old girl, Yella, who accounted for 26. This is the kind of difference in ability I would expect between a good, working, pure-bred deerhound and a genetically engineered exceptional all-round lurcher.

During the day, I also noted with interest the sociable relationship between my deerhound bitch and the hard working ferrets. Deerhounds, by dint of temperament, are very tolerant of smaller animals, with the exception of foxes. Gwen ignored the mustalid's presence whenever she was expected to do so and was intelligent enough to realise that when the same creature shook itself, then disappeared down that dark, fetid hole in the ground, it wouldn't be long before a rabbit bolted which she could chase.

People I meet at lurcher shows or correspond with often ask me about the ability of my working deerhounds when in pursuit of rabbits. Deerhounds will usually have to work twice as hard to look half as good as a lurcher in the class of Yella and I would categorise their skills in the same group as an average lurcher. Certainly I, or anyone known to me, would never perceive them to be a first choice as a rabbiting dog, but as long as I possess them, I will work them on any quarry available.

There are many deerhound owners who do not take the time to test their wards on this humble quarry, either by day when bushing or ferreting, or under the cover of darkness. My advice to these people is to give it a go. I guarantee they will not be disappointed and neither will their dogs.

Nora Hartley, a former stalwart of exhibition deerhounds, wrote in her book, *The Deerhound*, 'The hound does not seem to mind that its quarry is, so-to-speak, bastard to it, calling for a nimbleness which it often cannot produce.' The rabbit may not be the traditional prey of the Scottish deerhound. However the joy a hound finds in working this quarry must be witnessed to be appreciated.

Regular work on rabbits also helps maintain this aristocratic hound as a working breed at a time when many deerhound enthusiasts have relegated their dogs completely to the show arena.

A fine haul of over 40 rabbits was the result of our ferreting that day out on the fine Ray estate. Fortunately, this wily northerner did not lose his head on this ferreting trip, securing instead a crisp £5 note as a result of my bet with the farmer, although I almost had to prise it out of his hand. That will teach him to bet against a Doherty-bred deerhound.

CHAPTER 6

BLOODING THE YOUNG

Poignant memories of rearing our first ever litter of pure-bred deerhounds may have gradually faded into the past, but I still remember vividly how each one came into the world, blind and deaf, and how they struggled and squirmed to the warmth of their proud mother. Then as time passed, the siblings found their unsteady legs and played and tumbled, building up their strength for the big outside.

During that time we picked out two pups. They blossomed from wriggling whelps fighting for the best place for their mother's milk into rugged young deerhounds bounding along full of energy and fight.

The well thought out mating that begat this particular duo was our male deerhound Thorn (Shenval Isidore) mated to our Irish imported bitch, Gwen (Rosslyn Fling).

Thorn was bred in the land that gave rise to the breed. He was a product of the kennels of Pat Aird in Lanarkshire. We obtained this dog at a year old, and I doubt if his previous owner had ever taken the time to introduce him to the chase, but we soon put this right.

Within a month I had him jumping five-bar gates. In his first full season, he caught a fair number of rabbits and the odd hare. Thorn ran with a loping running style that could transform instantly to the all-out determination of a greyhound when he was on the back of a roe deer or fox. This male deerhound preferred chasing these larger creatures as opposed to rabbits.

Thorn killed foxes with ease. During his working time with me, he never required stitches as a result of injuries sustained tan-

The youngsters,
Lewis and Meg

gling with an angry fox. As soon as he saw a deer, he would be raring to go, his eyes out on stalks. He never gave in and would sometimes hit his prey with so much force the creature would be thrown into the air. I have seen roe deer lifted upwards with Thorn waiting for them to land. He would then pounce on them and the contest would be over.

Gwen, our foundation bitch, came to us from Brian Doak, a deerhound breeder who at that time we envied hugely because of the overall quality of his stock, whose consistent excellence was demonstrated within many litters. We considered Brian's strain to be a bitch line prepotent at producing quality, female deerhounds, so when an opportunity arose to secure a 12-week-old bitch pup we didn't hesitate for a minute. The importance of selecting high quality breeding females has been proven many times with most livestock and this was the quality we sought.

As our two pups from Gwen and Thorn developed, my father concluded they were of show quality and both youngsters attained major honours in puppy classes, at open and championship shows. It was also time for them to prove themselves in an arena more important to us: the hunt, which would cause them so much excitement and unleash their in-bred desire to chase.

Of the two youngsters, the bitch, Meg, possessed more scope than her brother, Lewis, both at show and in work. With most breeds of canine, bitches tend to mature earlier than their male siblings, both mentally and physically, and Scottish deerhounds are no exception to this rule.

So it was Meg I believed to be ready first for her maiden hunting outing. Like most of my young running dogs, this female was to be thrown unceremoniously into the night-time world of lamping. She would soon discover what it was like to work in inky black conditions with bobbing creatures coming and going like shadows on the grass in front of her.

Her initial prey of rabbits would serve to unlock the natural hunting instincts that, because of her tender age, were still dormant and relatively undisturbed.

Meg's ancestors were introduced to hunting with deer rather than the humble rabbit. These ancestors included Mr McNeill's famous deerhound, Buskar, who was born in the autumn of 1832 and, it is said, before he was a year old had killed a full-grown, red deer hind single-handed.

My bitch's first outing was a far cry from the hunting grounds of Mr McNeill's on the hills of Mar. Her stage was not steep hills and mountainsides, but rough grazing, untamed lands and ghylls overlooked by the famous 'Winter's gibbet', gallows on which hangs a wooden carved head representing William Winter, the last man to be publicly hanged in Northumberland.

I had visited and lamped this same area countless times. The farm for this hunting trip is not large by any means at around 350 acres, so it doesn't have the capacity to support rabbit populations in the same proportions as some of my much larger lamping grounds closer to the Anglo-Scottish border and beyond. The highest tally from any early season foray to this farm was 63 rabbits in one night. On other occasions I had secured numbers into the 50s. There are only a few brown hares living on this terrain, so when possible these are left for daylight excursions. Foxes are actually more numerous and I have taken many. Uniquely, the landowner has granted me permission to take roe deer, a consent of which I have taken full advantage.

Plantations of crossbill-filled Scots pine and siskin-infested Douglas fir, together with rough grazing pocked with molehills and plover-rich arable land well off the beaten track all contribute to a plentiful supply of creatures for sport. Season after season my team of lurchers and deerhounds have secured some excellent sport and vast hauls of rabbits from this area.

My training regime for building up puppy running dogs to the point of entering had seemed to work well with this deerhound. She was also well aware of what was expected of her in the way of retrieving, jumping and general obedience. Meg was also very keen, chasing anything that moved in front of her. Leaves blowing along tree-lined rides, plastic bags that danced a salsa on the wind and whirring partridge that lifted at the last possible moment in a grassed meadow would all be pursued with gusto. Her learning curve however had not, until now, included training with a beam of light.

My mid-week expedition started by walking through a paddock housing a 100 or so sheep. Meg lunged forward on seeing these giant cotton wool balls in front of her. I corrected her on this occasion, and on every other when she showed an interest, by jerking sharply on the leather slip leader around her neck. The last thing I wished was a dog that worried stock. In over 30 years of working running dogs, I have never possessed a dog with this fault, but pups tend not to adopt my rules automatically, so they must be discouraged and taught this imperative bylaw.

On into the next field, over a wire fence that tested my youngster's jumping ability and at last a number of rabbits were exposed by the pencil beam of light. Quickly I led my young hound directly to one particular rabbit that was quite undecided whether or not it should run or sit tight. This creature would have surely been number one in the bag for my old lurcher, Yella, but for a youngster, deerhound or otherwise, there is always that element of doubt.

Pups can make you long for a paracetamol sandwich at times. You are convinced they have detected the squatting rabbit caught in your beam, you excitedly release the dog only for it to run in the opposite direction. The rabbit is let off the hook, lifts and runs for safety. Your only hope is that none of your friends observed the embarrassing spectacle.

I led Meg to within five yards, but the rabbit decided enough was enough. It rose from its shallow resting place and ran in the direction of a fence line that was littered with recently felled branches. A good slip but awkward chase resulted, dog and rabbit dodging over and through an array of sawn obstacles. The youngster was not deterred in any way, and chased the rabbit with great determination, her jaws snapping like a man-trap every time her quarry's hindquarters came within striking distance. There was no mucking about with this gargantuan rabbit dog.

Alas, her evident keenness and determination were hampered on this occasion by a deficiency of experience. Good early work and some appalling bad luck meant the rabbit escaped down the entrance of a burrow. Meg stood with her head down the hole, scratching out sandy soil by the bucket-full with her front paws. Although such excavation work is not generally acceptable, I had to reward her running performance. Once I had sorted out her make-up of sand and dirt from around her eyes we proceeded further into the field.

Another revealing scan with my lamp saw more game around 20 yards out from the same fence. Some were squatting, while

The author lamping with Meg

others were already on the move. Instantly the dog pulled in the direction of the rabbits. Her dark, velvet ears were pricked and she panted with excitement. Meg's interest as a novice was direct-ed at the rabbits already running towards the fence that was their doorway to the field; her more experienced mentor, however, had other ideas. My sights were locked firmly on one particular rabbit I had singled out as her next potential victim and I hurried towards it as it lay flat and motionless in a shallow depression cre-ated by chunky tractor tyres.

This hunting trait of bypassing runners in areas where there is a large volume of rabbits is born of my experience of hunting nights where numbers are the dominant factor, but the same ploy is most useful for training pups when early success is paramount. There would be plenty of occasions later in this bitch's working career when runners, small numbers of lamp-shy rabbits and awkward runs would be the main features of a night's work.

Closer and closer we approached the rabbit, which twitched nervously with our every step. I was now practically shoving the dog's head in the direction in which the creature lay. The dog's mind remained focused on moving rabbits that were now behind us, her head battling to look in any direction other than straight forward. Suddenly our rabbit lifted – this triggered Meg's attention, which switched instantly to this individual. I released her as she pulled forward and the chase was on.

Into shadowy darkness the rabbit fled with Meg hot on its tail. Then, it made a couple of jinks in an attempt to try to shake off the dog and an almost 90 degree turn that took it back towards the fence. After loosing a bit of ground Meg once again caught up. The rabbit was closing on the fence and safety and at this point it was looking as if it would make it. But the dog put on a final burst and caught the rabbit with only a few yards to spare, grabbing it with a good strong hold across its back. Her first successful step up the hunting ladder had been achieved.

Another fundamental element of this deerhound's training was then put into practice as she retrieved her prey to my waiting hand. I rewarded her duly with a copious amount of praise. I split a hind leg of the rabbit and threaded it through the wide carrying belt of my battery pack. The slip was placed around the long neck of the eager pup, and we set off for another chase.

The rabbits in front of us were mainly on the move, constantly catching Meg's fervent attention. Deerhounds are very bright and pick up things they are interested in very easily and quickly. One rabbit under her belt doesn't constitute a great lamper, but I could see how this one kill had changed her. She seemed instantly more grown-up.

Across our path of illuminated tunnel vision dashed a rabbit I hadn't seen hiding. Without thought I clicked the deerhound into action, as if I had one of my experienced all-rounders with me. Meg burst from my side like a greyhound from the traps, splattering my face with cowshit as her back feet trod in a large pat. She made crossways for the rabbit which took her within striking distance and her head dipped down, but she missed her chance. The rabbit was making for a fair-sized hill, which housed the most established warren on the farm. Up the base of the mound it went and I kept the light trained on it, observing the chase from a fair distance. Meg seemed to zoom in and this time struck her prey well. Her brakes went on and even from afar I could make out the limp rabbit dangling from her jaws. With pomp, gliding grace and swishing tail she returned.

I allowed Meg to chase another half a dozen rabbits on this her maiden outing, adding two more to her final tally. These, together with the way she retrieved all her catches, came back in response to my call when she was unsuccessful or negotiated fences when she was let loose impressed me very much. At this point she was comparable with any young running dog I had ever brought on.

Were they here now, Meg's ancestors would no doubt be somewhat bewildered to see one of their type being entered onto such a diminutive adversary as the rabbit. But times have changed. In the next few decades, the same ancestors may be even more horrified, if all they observe is deerhounds coursing a lure due to the direction in which modern, poorly thought out and draconian legislation is going.

In the meantime, however, for this owner of working Scottish deerhounds, early success on rabbits will always be the order of the day – or, should I say, night!

CHAPTER 7

A STEP UP THE COURSING LADDER

Anumber of weeks passed since the fine autumn day when our deerhound bitch, Becky, was initiated into the competitive world of organised hare coursing. Not, I should add, as her new, main hunting discipline, more as another feature of her working repertoire. The time had come once again for her to prove her worth as a coursing deerhound, where the killing of the beast being pursued is not paramount.

Becky was one of the most loveable and sensible workers we possessed. When we were out together her finely-honed sense of smell and my sharp eyes always worked well. What I missed lying tightly hidden she would flush out, working enthusiastically like a spaniel to inform me of her new and interesting find.

Her maiden event had taken place amid the flat fen lands of Lincolnshire, with fields as big as deserts, where potential homes for yellow hammer and corn bunting have been ripped out. This land is actually what I would class as 'good going' for a running dog. The soil is soft, but lends itself to testing the stamina only, rather than the dog's different running skills and qualities. Most hares taken by dogs here have to be literally ground down, so the need is less for a fast, tight turning dog than for one that can follow and pick their time to strike. For organised hare-coursing purposes, using any breed, this type of land is ideal.

Becky's second bite at the 'coursing cherry' was to take place in a more difficult and dangerous landscape: ancient Scottish hills with flint-filled soil covered in varying lengths of coarse, tough heather. This is again an energy-sapping terrain where stamina and fitness are tested to the full, but so too are many other run-

An experienced deerhound coursing judge

ning qualities, including speed, sagacity and guile.

This uncultivated area also boasts vast expanses, but that is where any comparisons to the fens end. The moors are more picturesque compared to the softer, arable, southerly terrain, and there is a different overall feel to it. The landscape is filled with the evocative cries of curlews and the scent of flowering heather. The sense of history is almost tangible and I could easily imagine I heard the sharpening of spears on the stone walls of local churches as the ghosts of highland chieftains past prepared for battle.

The morning of the event was wrapped in a grey veil of gossamer-like fog which left a damp coating on everything it touched. The murkiness it created threatened to delay the beginning of the event, but as the mist cleared it exposed wildlife annoyed at our presence and land that rolled on forever towards the indigo horizon.

The thought of an area of land supplying 50 or so courses over two days may, at first, seem quite daunting. In this environment however, where man's interference hasn't, as yet, caused too much destruction or disease, large quantities of blue hares are always to be expected. So any one-day, 16 dog stake or two-day, 32 dog events should always be completed successfully, weather permitting. These moors are susceptible to sudden climatic changes. One moment the landscape can be smiling before you, then, in a flash, a wall of white mist drifts silently over the entire terrain, covering it with a thick white carpet in a matter of minutes. So, at the first sign of bad conditions approaching, any astute gamekeeper will immediately whisk hunting parties off to lower ground and safety.

Remarkably, spread over the first day of our hunting visit, we witnessed around 40 courses. Hares here at this time of year are almost pure white in colour. Because of this change, they are easy to spot lying among the dark heather and predators in the form of foxes, stoats and raptors with broad silent wings, are able to pick

A pair of deerhounds turning the hare

out resting hares that wrongly believe they are well concealed. The dogs also benefit, being able to maintain a better sight on their prey when in the throws of a twisting and turning course.

My first course of the day was with Becky's litter sister, Meg (Doxhope Lady Annadaille) who was also entered in the event. To be successful in competitive coursing, it goes without saying that the dog must have ability. However, that element we call luck will often play the nap hand. Luck on Meg's course was never forthcoming: she was unsighted when slipped and never able seriously to be an active part of the chase. I hate losing in this way, especially knowing the hunting pedigree of the bitch. Meg, like her sister, has taken a fair amount of hares, both blue and brown.

After another four courses by other contestants, it was Becky's turn. She was fitted into the dubbing-smelling, leather slip leader with her opponent. Both were walked steadily across the heather by the keen-eyed slipper, and it wasn't too long before a flash of pure white emerged from the ground.

I wouldn't be frightened to say that Becky's phenomenal take-off speed would see off most deerhounds in the country, not to mention a number of lurchers that I have witnessed. At the first turn, she led her opponent by eight clear lengths. She then began to clock up point after point as she twisted and turned with the hare. During most of this course, she did the entire work single-handed, with the other deerhound left in her wake. I still prayed he would not catch up. The last thing I needed was Becky running behind her coursing partner for the latter part of the chase, waiting for the hare to be turned onto her. She is pure deerhound but, at times, possesses all the cunning of a good cross-breed.

The course became a fairly lengthy affair, ending up at the other side of the only fence on the moors, which Becky cleared with ease. The same hurdle ended the course completely for her

Becky working the hare well next to the fence

non-jumping opponent. He was left a defeated spectator, jealously watching the conclusion of the chase with his head and shoulders sticking through the wires. The judge raised the red flag, indicating my bitch was through to the next round.

The competition progressed steadily through the main stake, until it was once again Becky's turn. This time that luck factor again deserted the Doxhope deerhounds. For a second time that day one of my hounds disappointingly lost the course through being unsighted from the slip.

It is difficult for people who have never hunted this terrain to understand how many courses are won and lost through dogs being properly or not properly sighted when slipped. Coursing on heather is a totally different ball game for dogs, slipper, judge and spectators. The slipper must determine when he believes both dogs have seen their quarry, this is not as easy as it would first seem, especially considering he is often being literally dragged across the heather by the dogs while struggling to keep his balance and footing.

It was announced that the first round losers' stake was to take place. It was Meg's turn once again. This time she got a good sight of the hare from the off. A good, lengthy course resulted. I believed it to have been a very close call before Meg took out the hare. Maybe I viewed the course with partisan eyes, or was wrong in my estimations, as her opponent took the honours. Meg carried the hare back, to a shout from behind me of 'go and get it from her Bill'. I scowled back in the direction of the line thinking, what's the point of training my dog to retrieve if I'm going to run out and take her catch from her, you stupid woman – the hare is caught, it's dead and the dog is demonstrating her retrieving ability. When she reached me, I said affectionately, 'Meg, you may have heard phrases shouted that contain no wisdom whatsoever. I hope you completely ignored them, as I did.' The dog looked up at me with a pleased look in her dark eyes. She might not have been able to understand what I had said, but her wagging tail suggested she agreed with the tone of my voice.

In the late afternoon, as the distant hills lay silhouetted against a steel-grey sky, it was again the turn of Becky, this time in the second round losers' stake.

At her previous coursing meeting, she was defeated by a deerhound from the famous Sorisdale kennels. On this occasion the result was to be reversed. She really showed her true ability and class on this course against a more experienced coursing deerhound. This was one particular coursing scalp that I had wished for very much.

Anyone connected with the breed will know what I mean when I say that deerhounds may sometimes turn a deaf ear, ignoring you completely. It seems this impolite trait can also be transmitted to their masters. No gentlemanly handshake or con-gratulations from the owner of the hound that Becky had just defeated. Never mind – she had won her way fairly and squarely into a semi-final on what was only her second event.

I was still full of delight at Becky's form as all the required courses were completed before darkness fell. I would have to wait till the following day to witness my bitch's display in the semi-final. Her confidence and ability were growing with every course. She was really on a roll. It would require a very good hound in-deed to defeat her at this stage. But, as with the semi-finals of any competition, all the competitors making it through to this stage would be good and anything could happen. However, I wouldn't be of Celtic descent if I didn't possess some form of lucky charm to help me along.

I owned a tweed jacket, handed down from my dad along with the tale that this garment was originally taken from the back of a scare-crow on Trevelion's estate near Netherwitton in North-umberland. The wearer would hardly be classed as a dedicated follower of fashion, as the coat had lost country-squire status long ago, but it slithered easily into place; it was comfortable and I al-ways felt I was wrapped in part of Scotland when I had it on. The cuffs were frayed and torn, buttons were missing and its scent wouldn't be out of place in a damp glade in any wood. To me, this was my lucky jacket. I wore it on many occasions, but mainly on my visits to Caledonia.

On the second day, we were lucky enough to be bathed in autumn sunshine once again. Grouse cackled from every quar-ter. The burn, near which I parked my Diahatsu Fourtrak, bub-bled along excitedly. Everywhere there was a vibrant *joie de vivre*. The waxed jackets of the previous day were replaced with short-sleeved body warmers and smart, chequered shirts. But my jacket hung in its rightful place.

I gathered from her boisterous antics that Becky was now in the mood. As we walked, soaking up the sense of the moors that surrounded us, she dragged me up every hill and mound with a total disregard for her owner's tiring legs. Her eyes scanned constantly for any sign of movement. Her radar-like ears were firmly pricked in anticipation of the cry of 'hare right' or 'hare left' and her nose sniffed and snorted the ground for scents.

The semi-final that had caused me to loose a night's sleep came around quickly. Again my hound was matched against a deerhound with not only a formidable show history but also a proven coursing record – Terichline Pipistrelle. This deerhound, although never to my taste aesthetically, had impressed me once or twice in the past with its running ability.

From the slips on this course, Becky again showed her phenomenal take-off speed. A swiftness from scratch that was too much for her opponent to match. Turn after turn Becky was continually in poll position ensuring an enormous haul of points. When her challenger did get into a position to pass her, Becky quickly overtook, these 'go-bys' adding even more points to her final tally. Becky won her way through to her first coursing final, far more easily than I could ever have anticipated, and once again I was on the receiving end of discourteous behaviour from a defeated owner.

Also making her way slowly but surely through the semi-final stages was Anastasia Noble's Ace. This deerhound, from the famous Ardkinglas kennel in Scotland, is one of Miss Noble's favourite hounds. Ace is also noted for speed from the slip and quickness to the hare, but maybe not for quality of coat, which could have easily fought my jacket for the scruffiest look. This final, on paper, possessed all the hallmarks of being a spectacle.

The hunting party trod the moor with military precision searching for a worthy hare. The slipper strained to keep the dragging pair together in front of him, as hares lifted and skipped across the heather, brave when a good distance lies between them and possible enemies. Suddenly a big strong looking hare lifted with just the right distance. A fair law for both hare and dogs was judged and both dogs were sighted and released.

Level pegging for the first 40 yards, these two sprint merchants quickly gained on the fleeing hare. One hell of a course took place, each hound sharing the workload, each of them having early opportunities to catch the hare. This was turning out to be a most plucky hare and the course rather lengthy and entertaining.

The older Ardkinglas hound's experience then started to show through. At times this meant my bitch was restricted to hanging behind, not able to bump her way past. Both dogs

Deerhounds coursing into the distance

had been equals during the first third of the chase, but Ace was beginning to win the second third.

In the latter stages Becky made one final attempt to take out the hare with an unsuccessful jaw-clapping strike. The hare on this occasion was strong and was not caught. Enough points however had been tallied by the eagle-eyed judge to award the flag in favour of Ace – a decision with which I could not disagree overall.

I chased after my keen bitch, which was unbelievably searching the air for the scent of another quick-footed hare to pursue. When fastened securely into her tether, the two of us strolled over to Darren Balloch, who was not only the slipper but also the custodian on the day of the winning hound. We exchanged a firm handshake and a 'well done' in acknowledgement of our enjoyment of the final. There are still some polite people within the ranks of organised coursing after all, I thought to myself.

Everyone attending agreed that this was probably the best of a trio of finals on the day. Any disappointment I had was, however, offset by the overall improvement of my bitch in every department. Her first event on the fens, with all its teething troubles, was now forgotten.

For me, Becky is a hunter, a freezer-filler. She runs hares, rabbit, fox and deer with all the cunning of the most experienced profit-hunter's lurcher. She catches these creatures for fun, and adapts well to all hunting situations. She would truly be a worthy addition to any lurcherman's team, or working deerhound person's kennel.

As a prolific hare courser, where points awarded decide the winner – only time will tell. But a final in her first season is one hell of a start!

And their hybrids

The author's Bes

CHAPTER 8

THE FIRST-CROSS DEERHOUND × GREYHOUND

I must begin my review of the virtues and short-comings of this cross by saying that I am by no means claiming it to be the ultimate longdog, far from it. Every hunter, every dog owner, requires something different from a dog, so for me to say that this cross is unsurpassed, would be an exaggeration. I do, however, consider that it is a very useful hybrid, not for a single, specialised type of hunting, but where dogs of all round ability are required, and it is possibly the most versatile of all the more common, first-cross F1 hybrids available in lurcher-dom.

The deerhound × greyhound is a most pleasing cross, and its temperament is similar in many ways to that of the deer-hound. Aesthetically, it shows its parentage well, and is exactly what would be expected from the union of these two pure-breds.

There can be a remarkable similarity of phenotype with deerhound × greyhounds, not only with siblings but also from litter to litter, probably more so than with any other first-cross progeny. The dog's actual frame is such that it might have been the original longdog and rarely are examples of this cross short-coupled or coarse.

A famous rhyme, which seems to have been adapted to eve-ry possible type of running dog over the decades – 'a neck like a drake, a head like a snake, a back like a beam, a chest like a bream, a foot like a cat, a tail like a rat' – actually fits the dog as if it had been created for it.

Bedlington × greyhound matings come close to matching

Four first cross deerhound greyhounds bred at Doxhope deerhounds.

such aesthetic consistency in their offspring, but in other first-cross progeny there can be a great deal of variation between individuals. The collie × greyhound, for example, can produce tall, smooth-coated, racy animals, small, heavy-coated, heavy-boned lurchers and coat pigments as varied as the wardrobes of mother nature, all in the same litter.

In the deerhound first cross, there is a quite consistent typical example or type, and the colours that are produced are also fairly constant. Genetically, there are only a small number of

90

possible colours that can be formed: these are brindle (in various shades) and also some blacks. The brindle coloration will always take precedence, no matter what colour of greyhound dam is used in the breeding. In well over 200 pups that my father and I produced from two main stud dogs, only five were black and these were all male. I do not mean to suggest that the black coloration is sex-linked. I am only conveying our findings.

I have heard it said that fawns could also turn up and I can see how this could possibly happen, for in the genetics of dogs it is generally accepted that mating brindle to brindle will produce a majority of brindles, with some fawns. But over many years of breeding longdogs and being involved with deerhound crosses, I have never seen an example. So the frequency, if any, must be extremely low. The genetics involved in the transmission of coat colour is truly complex and therefore still not fully understood.

The reason for such coloration in the deerhound × greyhound is because we are breeding together two dissimilar pure breeds. This is out-crossing: producing mongrels in fact. When this is done the law of heterosis is applied; that is creating animals with great vigour and stamina by burying or locking up recessive traits for one generation. It must however be remembered that these traits have only been arrested, not eliminated, so they are likely to recur in the second-cross or later generations. That is why in, say, the ¾ bred deerhound × greyhound × greyhound, or a first-cross deerhound × greyhound mated to any other lurcher composite a greater variation in colours will be seen.

What is classified as dominant and recessive in terms of colour pigments differs from breed to breed. In deerhounds, the dominant colour is actually brindle. In the greyhound brindle too is dominant, but so is black, and this is part of the reason why these two colours manifest themselves so much. But it is not only coat pigments that are affected through heterosis: any recessive shortcoming will also be masked by hybrid vigour.

STRUCTURE AND FEET

I have always been a great advocate of the need for working dogs to be as sound as possible, as I believe a dog cannot fully achieve its potential as a worker if it is being hampered by one or more structural faults. Granted, there will have been many examples of dogs that didn't conform to what is considered structurally correct but still went on to be good workers, but how much better would these have been had they not had floored limbs, bone or muscles. Structural faults do not get better or lessen with age either.

Feet are a part of the running dog that is extremely important to me as a hunter and, as a rule, the feet of deerhound × greyhounds meet my requirements. They are in the main very durable, being able to withstand measureless volumes of work and the most hostile of grounds. I have worked my first crossers and have observed many others in Northumberland and on the Scottish borders where the ground is what would be categorised as harsh. So if these dogs can cope here, it puts them in good stead to work with minimal injuries in any other location in Great Britain.

I have worked two deerhound first crossers kept back out of those we bred and between them experienced only one jumped toe in over a decade. When I say worked, I do not mean venturing out on odd occasions but rather pure, unadulterated graft: lamping excursions from one o'clock in the morning till dawn then switching to daylight work on strong, Scottish Border hares or roe deer. Our dogs worked first shift, night shift

Merlin, a first-cross deerhound × greyhound

and back shift, every week of the year.

With such arduous exertion, a dog with poor feet would certainly be found wanting and would be of little value to the more serious workers of running dogs, no matter how good its other abilities and hunting prowess made it. It would be like possessing a super fast sports car with four flat tyres.

I remember hearing the owner of a saluki × greyhound stating, 'It's a great dog on hares, but he gets injured every time I take him coursing.' What use is a dog like this? It certainly would not fit my ideal as a hunting companion, nor would I allow it room in my kennel.

The ideal feet on a dog are what I term 'button feet', which are tight and neat in appearance with short strong nails, making the dog look as if it is up on its toes when standing. How a dog's foot looks, however, is sometimes of no consequence. I have seen such feet causing nothing but bother for some dogs, while others with long toes and nails that scream out 'these are going to be trouble', went unscathed. But on the whole, it is the button type of foot that I strive for.

Not every first-cross deerhound × greyhound can have great feet and there will certainly be individuals even within this circle of dogs that do possess a more injury-prone foot. This can be attributed to many factors, including the parents, for it has been proved that such a trait can be passed on from one generation to another. Breeders using working types of deerhound tend to produce stock with good, hard feet. Those using show deerhounds, however, may have less success in this important department. I believe that many of the purebred deerhounds with which our stud dogs, Thorn and later his son Lewis, were mated were brought to us to correct the bitch pup's bad feet. I remember one lady who gasped when Lewis entered the compound.

'My god look at those feet,' she squealed enviously.

Certainly a lot of greyhounds have trouble with their feet, but it is not surprising when we observe the way in which these dogs perform and the extreme pressures put on their bones and tendons.

External factors can also influence the final outcome of how a dog's foot will perform when tested in a working situation. These can range from too much or too little exercise when young, incorrect diet, lack of calcium, too few or too many vitamins and nails being too long. These cannot be blamed on the dog, and I have witnessed some of the so-called experts of lurcherdom bemoaning a certain breed or individual animal, condemning them for having bad feet, when in fact the shortcoming was due to the dog being kept locked up in a small kennel all day and every day, then, on the odd occasion when it was taken out, expecting it to do the business.

Therefore as an overall basis of comparison, the average first-cross deerhound × greyhound will have feet as good as, and in some cases better than, most other first-cross composites.

SCENTING AND NOSE WORK

Everyone will probably have heard the old music-hall gag:

'My dog has no nose.'

'But how does it smell?'

'Bloody terrible.'

The statement that a dog has 'no nose' seems to find its way regularly into various lurcher publications and many times I have seen it applied to the deerhound and hybrids bred from it. The implication is that deerhounds possess little or no olfactory sense to speak of.

A lurcher cross of any breeding may be unique in many respects, but all dogs have certain things in common. All possess the same number of bones, all have the same number of teeth, every dog is regarded as being colour blind and all seem to have excellent hearing and smell. The latter senses have evolved over a long period of time and have been harnessed by man.

It is thought all dogs evolved from the predatory Tomarctus that lived 15 million years ago. From this creature, four early canine types evolved: *Canis familiaris metris-optimæ*, the precursor of sheep-herding breeds; *Canis familiaris intermedius*, the ancestor of various hunting, hauling and toy breeds (the latter descended from Egyptian house dogs); *Canis familiaris leineri*, responsible for the sight hounds, also for many terriers; and the last of the quartet, *Canis familiaris inostranzewi*, which has given us powerful mastiff-type animals as well as some of our water dogs. Many of today's breeds are results of crossing the ancestral animals that came down from these four basic canine types.

Then, as the union between man and his best friend developed, so crude selections were made for type and the canine species began to be formed into utilitarian breeds. Dogs were developing for specific purposes, to aid men in hunting, in war, and as herders, pets and companions. Up to recent times, with the use of genetic tools, *Canis familiaris* has been diversified to such a fantastic degree, only genealogical knowledge now assures us of the link between dogs and their feral ancestors.

I reiterate that the lurcher is a unique breed, but its distinctiveness does not include a poor sense of smell – this includes dogs bred from the union of a deerhound and a greyhound. The real question here is exactly what the lurcher owner requires from the nose of his hunting companion.

I have hunted with lurchers for many decades, beginning long before the advent of lamping as we know it. In those early days dogs were expected to hunt by sight and by scent. Observing your dog working through long grass, scrub or bushes on the scent of a hare, fox, deer or rabbit produced as much of a buzz as watching the same dog scanning field or fell for movement, or indeed the actual chase itself. With every deerhound × greyhound I have owned, good nose work, although never the major priority, has always been an important element of my hunting requirements.

SPEED, STAMINA AND AGILITY
The deerhound × greyhound certainly gives the impression of being a real speed merchant, and in most cases this impression is borne out. These dogs are half greyhound of course so they are more than capable of matching the swiftness of the best hares. Fox, deer and rabbits will also be defeated in the contest of speed.

Dogs of this breeding run with so much effort and determination, and again, if we compare them with other first-cross contemporaries for speed, they will be up there among the leaders.

I once visited friends over the border many years ago, and these boys were devotees to first-cross greyhound × whippets. On our first night-time outing I was truly amazed at the sheer take-off speed these crosses possessed. They were also quite nimble on the turn, but after a short period of time, and with only a couple of courses under their belts, their owners were preparing for the homeward journey. The deerhound lurcher and first-cross deerhound × greyhound bitch accompanying me were just getting warmed up. Any incredible turn of speed my Scottish acquaintances' dogs possessed, quickly waned as the night progressed. Speed is a necessity, but excessive speed is not the be-all and end-all some folk would have us believe.

As well as having enough speed, deerhound × greyhounds are fairly well endowed with stamina. Maybe not the same staying power that has composites bred from its Arabian cousin reportedly running fen hares for four, five or even six minutes, but stamina to run one or two minutes flat out. The Caledonian dog also possess great powers of recovery, so a good number of chases can be attained over a day or night's sport and probably be repeated the following day and the day after that.

The blend of speed and stamina was the main factor that caused these crosses to be the ultimate, hare-coursing dogs for most of the 70s. At this time, matching, where the object is killing hares rather than coursing, took place in all counties. The zestful deerhound × greyhounds suited many regions where smaller fields abound and anywhere where the running dog must get to the hare quickly. Nearly 20 years later and the fens where discovered: at last a use for the saluki × greyhound, which up till then hadn't shown as much running diversity as the deerhound × greyhound. I believe it was this vast terrain, not the competition between the two crosses, that was to end an era of deerhound × greyhound supremacy as match dogs.

A third asset for a running dog is agility, and I must admit that I do like to see sharpness and tightness. The average deerhound × greyhound would never be classed as sharp. I keep this adjective for my smaller deerhound lurcher stock, which can grab a low flying partridge out of the air or take rabbits and hares from their seats. The first-cross deerhound × greyhound does however possess a fair amount of agility and nimbleness for such a large cross: enough to get down to the most awkward rabbit, or throw itself at the strongest hare. Again it boils down to which deerhound × greyhound it is and how it was bred. Our stock tended to be, on average, smaller and therefore fleeter than those fine examples produced by other creators of the cross.

JUMPING

Deerhound F1 hybrids absolutely love to jump and they are incredible athletes in this department. We had an aphorism in Northumberland when I was younger – 'no jumping, no hares' – a saying to which I still religiously adhere. All my dogs jump, and this includes the pure deerhounds. It is an easy discipline for dogs to learn, and when they master the basics, not only do they enjoy it, but they give this owner immeasurable pleasure watching them perform.

I start my deerhound × greyhounds' jumping training from an early age, at around six to 10 weeks. This is not jumping the garden fence or five-bar gate heights I must add; rather it consists of me placing one or two lengths of wood around the runs where the pups are exercised. These bars are only three or four inches high, too low for the youngsters to clamber under, so they more or less have to step over them. This imprints the idea of getting over an obstacle into their young heads, not to clear enormous heights – this comes later in life, when joints and muscles have fully developed.

As they grow, so too does the height of the hurdles and the type of obstacle is also altered. Anything is utilised at this stage, even rolls of wire mesh or old doors. By using dissimilar objects there is less chance of conditioning the dog to jump only one particular hurdle. I have seen dogs that jumped wooden fences with ease, but dithered at post and wire, or dry-stone walls.

Jumping training can also assist in early retrieving schooling – in fact killing two birds with one stone, as dummies are thrown over a barrier for the dog to bring back. Deerhound first crosses, and lurchers produced from them, tend to be natural retrievers of game, so with only a little aid they can become quite competent.

I once owned a 27-inch deerhound cross dog called Fly. I trained this lurcher up to exceptional standards, as I wanted a dog that retrieved well at all costs. Fly carried anything, fruit, eggs, birds, tins of larger; even the post that came through the letter box was brought to me at the command of 'fetch'. I won many rosettes and trophies at lurcher shows with Fly, and in the fields he brought back rabbits, hares and even foxes that he killed. As a jumper he was a natural, and no obstacle was too high for him. A seven-foot baton fence that surrounded local allotments was scrabble-jumped, much to the amazement of the gardeners digging and hoeing their plots.

COMPANIONSHIP
As a pet or companion, deerhound × greyhounds are what I deem 'safe'. The excellent temperament of the Scottish deer-

hound seems to take precedence over the unpredictability of the greyhound, especially with smaller dogs. They are never 'shy biters' as many collie first crosses can be and they can be trusted implicitly with children.

Because of its genotype, the deerhound × greyhound is very human orientated, sometimes preferring the company of people to that of other dogs, and they are always so eager to please. They possess a huge amount of affection and love to be cuddled. Truly a lovely dog and a joy to own.

SHOWING

Lurcher shows are another part of our hobby that seems to cause argument at the very mention of them. Some people love them, a lot of folk hate them. For myself, I think they are great, the window to our breed for those outside lurcherdom to come and see what all the excitement is about. Shows are also natural meeting places for friends, both old and new.

However they are perceived, it must be remembered they are, in the main, a bit of fun, a canine beauty competition, and it is one person's opinion (the judge) as to which dogs are considered the best, but only on how they look and are presented.

Deerhound × greyhounds tend to do well at these exhibitions, even when under the scrutiny of men who prefer other crosses. These dogs are good lookers and certainly give the impression of being the part. Whether or not they are is a matter of testing them in the field but, on the day of the show, it is what they look like and how they are put together that counts.

I travel the length and breadth of the country visiting lurcher shows and game fairs each year, and whether I am judging, showing or just there to make up the numbers, I enjoy them

Deerhound greyhounds usually do well at shows

now just as much as I did when I visited my first, run by the Shildon Gun Club in County Durham during the 70s.

THE DEERHOUND × GREYHOUND – A FINAL WORD

In this chapter, I have attempted to provide the reader with a candid evaluation of the first-cross deerhound × greyhound, borne from my extensive experience in keeping, breeding and working them.

I have covered many aspects of the dog in order to help people simply wishing for more information and to assist those considering keeping this cross to make up their minds whether this is the one for them. As I believe these animals have much more to offer other than their working attributes, I have also commented on their virtues as companions.

The F1 deerhound × greyhound may not be everyone's cup of tea, but then again, which cross is? It is a composite that can differ in ability according to the type of parents used in the breeding, not only according to the working type of the deerhound parent – which I have emphasized constantly – but also according to the genes of the greyhound parent. Some say coursing greyhounds are the better producers, others opt for track animals. To me it is of no consequence: all greyhounds are keen. They are determined killers that will tear to shreds whatever they catch, whether it be fur or rag, and the difference between a winning and losing greyhound is measured sometimes in only 100ths of a second. The vital choice my father and I made was always to go for sounder greyhound bitches in our breeding plans, dogs that rarely needed a sick note because of injuries to muscles, bones and feet. I was lucky to have many friends and contacts in the land of my forefathers, from whom I have obtained some great Irish-bred greyhounds over the years.

The deerhound × greyhound is a very useful cross for hunters that want to try their hand at pursuing everything. It is a British dog, bred for British countryside and terrain, having a weather-proof coat that will keep out the coldest wind and a tough, durable skin which does not tear easily and which protects against the sharpest thorns.

All in all, a very versatile cross.

CHAPTER 9

DEERHOUND LURCHERS

Over the years, many astute lurcher breeders and perceptive hunters have noticed that a greater degree of hunting diversity could be obtained by the introduction of genes from various breeds or crosses to any first cross. These observations are not restricted to any one particular breed of lurcher, but for the purpose of this book and because of my experience and expertise, deerhound-blooded lurchers are highlighted.

A common term brandished about for such dogs, but not by me, is bitzas, that is having a bit of this and bit of that in their ancestry. Such a name doesn't do these versatile lurchers any justice, and implicit in it is the suggestion that they are mistakes with no thought having gone into their creation, when in fact, many were far from accidental. Indeed, in certain situations much deliberation went into their production, probably more so than with any first-cross mating. I prefer to identify them as 'all-rounders'.

However, along with any additional diversity that appeared from this breeding technique, came a larger degree of variation not only in phenotype – what the dogs look like – but also in performance and structural soundness. Within the litters from this breeding method, some progeny will resemble deerhound crosses. At the other end of the scale, a number will look like whippet crosses, and there will be various other shapes, sizes and possible breed comparisons in-between. Some of these animals will make good rabbiting dogs, others first-rate hare coursers but, as sure as the sunrise, the majority will make useful all-rounders, Jacks-of-all-trades.

A good cross section of deerhound lurchers

An explanation of the complex genetics of reproduction that results in the diversity of these litters is beyond the scope of this book. However, a simple explanation is useful.

Every dog possesses 39 pairs of chromosomes. Chromosome numbers differ in other creatures: fruit flies for example have 8 pairs, whereas human beings possess 46 pairs.

Chromosomes are like storage boxes where genes are held. Genes contain the material on which specific traits are built and which will determine the progeny's characteristics, including what it will look like, how big it will be, what colour it will be and so on.

So both the male and female dog have 78 chromosomes, or storage boxes each. In each one of these there are about 100,000 genes, which equals 78 × 100,000 genes per dog. In a mating, the chromosomes of the parents separate and half of the genes from the sire unite with half from the dam, and a new individual is created.

This means that both parents have contributed one half or their genes to each puppy in the litter. The genes to make up the half passed on by either of the parents are selected at random. We must also remember that a male dog produces about 600 million sperm in one mating. It takes only one of these sperm to fertilise an egg, and no sperm, or egg, carries exactly the same genetic material as any other. Another relevant fact is that each parent received their genes from their own parents, so it is possible that genes that the sire obtained from his father could be passed on to a puppy. When this happens, the pup may be more like his grandfather than its father. This mixing of genes is why we see such a variation from lurcher to lurcher matings.

Deerhound lurchers can range from ¾ bred deerhound × greyhound × greyhounds, to any dog with at least some deerhound in its ancestry, and it is the degree of deerhound in the dog that can dictate how versatile it will be. For example, deerhound greyhounds × saluki greyhounds in my experience can be useful animals. Deerhound greyhounds × collie greyhounds can make great hunters and deerhound greyhounds × Bedlington greyhounds, as a rule, are excellent all-rounders. I have also seen some individuals that on paper were around ⅛ deerhound and in the field were 'crackers'.

This also demonstrates that the dogs I refer to as all-rounders can also have one or more breeds in their ancestry that help to produce hunting diversity. I believe the versatility of a lurcher will peak with a maximum of three or four breeds in its genetic make up. We have all seen advertisements such as deerhound/greyhound/collie/saluki × Bedlington/whippet/border terrier/Afghan lurchers for sale. These make me question whether the vendor is being facetious with some underlying warped sense of humour. If not, these animals could possibly make useful all-rounders, but I believe with less consistency, and I would be very dubious of acquiring an example for myself. *Caveat emptor*, let the buyer beware.

During the 70s, probably the best lurcher living in mid to north Northumberland was Ron Murray's dog, Thorn, nicknamed 'the Assassin'. Thorn was bred from a first-cross deerhound × greyhound, mated with a local lurcher × lurcher bitch which also had some deerhound in her genetic make up, plus some collie. This dog remains a legend in the town of Ashington and outlying areas and he possessed formidable versatility on all quarry.

My lurcher bitch, Bes, was begat from the same sire as Ron Murray's exceptional dog, but this time he was mated to another bitch from the area, noted for her intelligence and stamina: Loopy, owned by Phil Jamison from Choppington near Bedlington. I continued a line from Bes till the seventh generation of lurcher × lurcher matings, before going back to an element of the rootstock, in the form of a sound track greyhound.

Ron Murray's dog, Thorn, the Assassin

These, and dogs of similar breeding permutations, became some of the best all-rounders in the county at that time, inheriting such desirable traits from their mixed ancestors as grit and stamina from the deerhound, intelligence from the collie and speed and determination from the greyhound. Due to an abundance of game in Northumberland, lurchermen have always required a more versatile type of dog, and these crosses certainly fitted the bill, probably more so than any other composite before or since. I have been most fortunate to have lived in a time when this class of lurcher ruled the roost.

These lurchers, bred-down from dogs originally from larger stock, produced running dogs that suited so many hunters. In size, bitches levelled out between 23 and 25 inches on average, weighing around 40 to 50lbs, ideal dimensions for the all-rounder. Dogs were slightly bigger in every department, but a 27-inch dog at that time would be classed as big; not too big mind you: as has been said many times before, 'it's not so much the size of the dog, but what it has inside that counts.' I couldn't agree more.

The 70s was a period of major change in the world of lurchers, an exciting time. Never before had dogs undertaken such large volumes of work, and more importantly, passed with flying colours, not just on what had been, until then, the main prey of rabbits and hares, but on fox and roe deer too. Lamping was born, and the top working dogs were being hunted frequently, sometimes up to five nights a week and with other forms of hunting in-between. How the countryside of my native Northumberland supported enough game to satisfy all the keen hunters and new breed of lurcher is beyond me.

As part of my breeding plan, and a premise of maintaining their many virtues, I always mated a rough to a smooth: the equivalent of pairing yellow to buff in the bird world. I believe

The author's Bes, a second-generation deerhound lurcher

that continual pairing of smooth to smooth will eventually produce progeny that are too fine for serious all-round work, and the mating of rough to rough will cause the stock to become too coarse and cloddy. My assertion worked to a degree, and I produced stamina-packed deerhound lurchers that were not only quick and agile, but possessed the temperament required for the vast amounts of work we gave them.

I have already stated that I could never vouch for the first-cross deerhound × greyhound as the ultimate longdog. I could however, without fear of any criticism whatsoever, say that deerhound-blooded lurchers have been the best crosses I've witnessed as all-rounders in my lifetime. They are certainly the most suitable for the varied work I have always participated in, on the harsh, game-abundant terrain where I hunt, the wild lands of Northumberland and the Scottish Borders.

An anthology of
true hunting stories using my lurchers

CHAPTER 10

THERE'S LIFE IN THE OLD DOG

My 1999 rabbit catching season was fully under way, when once again I began to crave the excitement of the nocturnal sport of lamping. All the expedients I used to secure fruitful and enjoyable hunting seasons over several decades had left me with many memories of rousing days and stirring nights.

September, and the appearance of autumnal colours, had stolen upon us. Although a time when the countryside begins to prepare for its annual slumber, September can also bring vastly different climatic conditions, capable of drying up wells or breaking down bridges. For me as a hunter, September signifies the true commencement of my favourite sport. While August can provide the aspiring lamper with an abundance of rabbits, these are in the main 'green', as yet uneducated to the dangers lurking behind the hunter's beam. Such rabbits are ideal quarry for youngsters or aged lurchers or for building up the fitness of the owner's best lamping stock. More testing prey comes later, from September till the turn of the year.

My dogs here at Chateaux Doxhope were once again beginning to fulfil their destiny, proving their worth in the hunting field. Limited graft combined with the appealing, but not energetic, activities of summer shows and our breeding programs had left the dogs lacking the hardness and fitness required for arduous nights out lamping rabbits. Lamping involves almost every resource of the dog being used, so dropping out-of-shape individuals into the lamping arena can be a catalyst for disaster, increasing the chances of injuries and leading to long-term physical short-comings or even fatalities.

The author and Yella, with her 57
rabbits in one night's work

As far as I am concerned, there are only two weights for a running dog, the correct weight and the wrong weight. At the beginning of this 1999 campaign, I would have definitely categorised my dogs as drifting towards the latter, being a bit too heavy. In an attempt to rectify this, I increased my tried and tested regime of road walking and 'balling' in the local fields. I have chosen to train all my lurchers and deerhounds to retrieve balls or sticks that are thrown for them, so I can easily adapt this playful activity into a most useful form of fitness training. I also slowly added the hunting discipline of lamping to gain sharpness as well as overall fitness.

I must admit there was a time in my life when I lamped all year round, driven by an insatiable appetite to be out hunting with my faithful dogs, a fire that the waters from all the seas in the world could never quench. But as I get older, it is usually August when lamps and batteries are brought out. Early season forays do, however, lend a hand in removing those unwanted pounds, and I have seen dogs with backs on take part in a few lamping excursions amid large numbers of rabbits and quickly begin to resemble skeletons.

For those not *au fait* with me as a hunter, I consider myself a serious lamper, defining myself as 'consistently taking large volumes of game many times a month'. The accurate records

I have kept religiously, not just over many years but over decades, show that on occasion I have lamped up to 20 times over a four-week period. From other pages, I uncover that between 400 and 500 rabbits were taken in that same period, in most situations, between a small group of dogs. This volume of work cannot be achieved safely unless dogs are fit and healthy.

It was at the beginning of this season when Steven Carr, a lurcherman from neighbouring County Durham, suggested a night's lamping. Steve was the co-owner of Old Molly's Bedlingtons. His prodigious knowledge and awareness of lurchers, plus his commonsense approach and views on running dogs, were respected by fellow lurchermen from both sides of the Tyne. Although maybe not a profit hunter like me and other members of my team, Steve still enjoys regular outings with dog and lamp. So the organised evening's sport was more of a social event than an effort to obtain large numbers of rabbits.

On the night I took along my sagacious lurcher, Yella, a ten-year-old bitch. Steve's lurcher was also a bitch, called Tilly; at the age of seven she too would have been classed as a veteran, but 'if they're good enough, they're young enough'.

These two oldies, due to sheer volume of work in the past, were very much time-wounded and scarred – unlike the third canine member of our team, a sapling lurcher named Adda, a black first-cross deerhound × greyhound bred from my deerhound stud, Lewis, and a well-bred greyhound bitch obtained from my good friend, Tom Squires, in Ireland.

Those patient designers and sculptors, time and experience, have moulded Yella into a great all-round lurcher, bettered out of the dogs I've owned only by her grandmother, Bes. Her specialist rabbit-taking prowess makes her the best rabbiting dog I've bred and kept. This bitch was primarily a nocturnal hunter of coney, but late in her career I reservedly entered her into daylight rabbiting, to which she adapted with ease. She was a lurcher that never knew what it meant to give in. Yella, at this advanced age, had also produced a litter of strong, healthy puppies during the summer months, to carry on my breeding line.

A short while prior to our night-out, this old bitch took 30 rabbits in one night's work. So she is far from being finished as a lamping dog, or indeed set to be thrown onto the canine scrap-heap as a brood bitch. She had also recently been entered in a lamping competition run by the Northumberland and Durham Working Lurcher Club, so she really demonstrates the truth of the adage, 'you are never too old'.

Young Adda, on the other hand, is near the beginning of his learning curve, and quite unique in my kennels. I am primarily a bitch man as I find these are more loyal and easier to train. I have rarely kept head-strong, stopping-at-every-lamppost-for-a-piss, male lurchers, but I reserved him because I have always had a gift for picking a good pup and he took my fancy in one of our litters. As yet, Adda doesn't know what it is to have run 50 rabbits in less than an hour then be slipped onto a lively hare, or to run on unthawed ground or deep furrows of soil. But he does know me and senses from the tones in my voice what is expected from him, trotting contentedly at my side wherever I go.

This sapling was at a time in his career, and more important-ly at the stage of development, when he should be obtaining his first kill. On this excursion, this is what I was hoping for with him. I do like early success for all my pups.

I always work on the premise of introducing young running dogs to rabbits first, then slowly working them onto the more difficult hare. As their age, experience and ability increases they are steadily introduced to deer and fox, not because I believe these are better creatures to chase, but they do require a skill and strength that is usually acquired with age.

There is a piece of interesting history behind Steve's dog, Tilly, and Steve plunged into the story. Bill Smith, a lurcher-man from Kingston Park near Newcastle upon Tyne, gave Tilly to Steve when her litter brother, Strike, was lost through injury. Such generosity is typical of more genuine lurcher folk. I hadn't previously seen this lurcher working but, knowing Steve, I knew she must be something special. Good dogs are always kept, rarely are they sold on or disposed of simply because they are getting on in years.

We used one of my farms for this night out. This is game-a-plenty land, where I controlled the moles during the spring and during hostile winters helped manage the ground game, musky-smelling chicken thieves and a few straying roe deer. The environment also lends itself well to housing a fine array of bird-life, from buzzard to goldcrests, from hawfinches to hoo-poes, and I had visited the location many times on bird watching outings.

On our arrival, Steve's Transit van – not designed for such off-road excursions – rumbled slowly along the overgrown, grassy lane and through a series of crystal-clear fords. We prepared under the glow of the van's cab light, pulling on leggings, fastening wide battery straps and checking connections on lamps. From the branches of trees hidden in the twilight, a tawny owl broke the silence with its long, wavering, eerie call.

Once ready we began our task and discovered that the resident rabbits were not, as we had hoped for, feeding in great numbers on the lush, open pastures. Most were lying amid the prickly, uncut thistle beds.

When lamping for numbers in places dotted with such patches of thistle, we would usually walk through these with our lurchers off their leads. The dogs are then expected to work out, chase and catch any quarry put up and caught in the swishing beam of light. This is where a good understanding between lamper and dog is paramount, as it can make all the difference in the final analysis on the night. This outing however was less numbers orientated, so we decided to make do with any rabbits we saw on more open ground.

My bitch Yella accounted for the first rabbit. The creature lay motionless behind a small clump of grass. I slinked towards it as kamikaze moths threw themselves at the glass lens of my lamp from all sides. This is a feature of early season lamping for which you must be prepared. At times you either get stoned or eaten alive by angry winged insects that are attracted to your light.

The uneasy rabbit lifted, instantly at full speed, and bolted in the direction of a well-established field warren. I remember ferreting these exposed holes, which were decked with a bewildering array of footprints, scratchings and scents at the back end of the previous year and obtaining quite a good tally of rabbits.

Yella tracked her prey like a shadow. Her speed and agility prevented the creature entering one of the many chasms of its home. After a number of unsuccessful attempts to find a hole and safety from a lurcher with over 2000 rabbits to her credit, the rabbit was eventually picked up as it dived behind one of the staggered smaller thistle patches. That was number one in the bag for the night.

The next few rabbits chased were excellent, running like bobbing cyclones over short distances, trying everything in their power to shake off the stronger, faster dogs. This jinking and turning would probably have thwarted lurchers of lesser ability and experience than our two oldies. Some people in the lurcher world wrongly think rabbits are 'easy to catch'. Granted, in some instances they can be, but in other situations they can demonstrate just as much agility as the wiliest hare. One such gutsy rabbit tried every manoeuvre possible to shake off the attentions of Steve's keen bitch.

After some good runs and another couple of rabbits caught, we arrived at the entrance to a large silage field, the rickety gate to which creaked and groaned as we opened it. I gave Steve the details about the shape of the field and directed him where to go, and we split up. The harvest of grass had recently been cut and collected, a late second cutting of the year that had left the ground cracked and very hard. In this situation the difficulties associated with catching a rabbit or hare can be magnified. Dogs rarely perform well on this ground: most make only half-hearted attempts when turning with their prey. In fact, I have witnessed dogs belonging to others not running at all. In this field, however, I saw from a distance what I classed as the rabbit chase of the night.

A long slip of Tilly by Steve, on a rabbit already on the move, saw the bitch doing a lot of work up and down a fence line. Numerous times she kept the creature from making its escape from the field. Most of the chasing was done going away from the lamp, this adding to the awkwardness of the course. The rabbit jinked and dodged in front of the dog's snapping jaws. Then in the distance, at the very tip of the beam, we heard the noise signifying the rabbit was caught. This was followed by an impressive retrieve by Tilly.

Sometimes some lurchermen, for various reasons, consider that rabbits and even hares deserve to get away if they have performed well. On the other hand, if the dog has given its best during a chase I must admit I hate to see the quarry escape, especially if it's a young dog learning its trade.

Speaking of young dogs, under the power of my lamp Adda was to account for his first kill. I pinpointed a squatting rabbit and led him close enough to see before it lifted from its seat. My youngster pulled forward and I released him from his tether and he was off like a dog possessed. A striding, but good turn of speed, took him quickly up to his prey. He struck at the creature with venom, locking it in his powerful jaws. This tremendous strike and the speed at which he travelled caused him to summersault but still hang on to his first rabbit. The subsequent retrieve to my hand by the pup was my reward for all those early training sessions.

In the same field, my youngster ran another couple of rabbits. These both just made it to the sanctuary of their homes before he could catch them, even though he did strike at them well and his superior speed had won the race against them. While in the throws of coursing a third rabbit, the dog hit some farm machinery. The painful, but not too serious injury was to curtail his evening's sport, and the remainder of his evening was used to walk off the bruising and to watch and learn from his mentors.

At the farm's walled and double-fenced boundary, our lamps beckoned each other and Steve and I met up, allowing ourselves time to ponder what we had already witnessed. We sat on the baked ground as the three dogs sniffed their welcomes. The night had been pre-planned, but unfortunately we couldn't pre-plan the weather and at no time was it text-book lamping conditions. The black plantation edges were silhouetted against a dark-purple sky and the drone of car engines drifted from the distant, winding, country roads.

After our break, we stayed together pushing through the next part of our journey, with all the dogs fastened, taking turns to run the two elders. It was Yella's turn once again and, believing we wouldn't be racing many more that evening due mainly to the poor conditions, I slipped her on a set of reflecting eyes that glared back at us from the middle of the field. As the experienced lamping dog she is, Yella paced herself out down the beam of light towards the squatter like a collie creeping to round a pack of sheep then, in the last couple of yards, she accelerated for the kill. As she struck, I saw it wasn't a rabbit that lifted but a large, leggy hare, the only one we had seen that evening.

I have never been someone who believes it is unsporting to course hares on the lamp: they are very capable athletes and can look after themselves, and I race them whenever the occasion arises. As with rabbits, however, I rarely lamp hares with more than one dog, as the chance of a collision is greatly increased in the darkness.

Yella was now on the back of the hare, and there was nothing I could do about it. If I had switched the lamp off, she would have pursued her prey in the dark. She whipped the creature all over the place, turning and twisting a yard behind it. Even in her prime, Yella was rarely used on hares. Her forte, because of what I required of her in hunting, was large numbers of rabbits, so the last thing I needed for her at a decade old was the chase of a strong Northumberland hare.

The course went on and on. Anyone who didn't know the dog would have wondered how this old timer could be doing so well. Steve slipped Tilly, either in excitement or because he thought she could lend a helping hand. Now both the experienced members of our team were up and running on the same beast. Between them the dogs worked this strong, but at times lucky, hare.

Social lamping for the time was forgotten, as Steve and I took turns illuminating the chase, depending on who was closest at the time. Two lamps switched on at the same time can be counter-productive, at times blinding the dogs.

There were a number of occasions when either bitch might have caught the hare, but slowly and surely the creature's plan began to work. After gradually taking the chase towards the fence, it made its escape under the bottom rung of the three strand wire fence and into the plantation.

The two dogs, as one can imagine, returned tired and panting heavily. I was disappointed and felt for the two. My feelings, however, were not embarrassment, far from it, as in their younger days either would probably have taken this hare out single-handed.

After another welcome break for tired dogs and excited owners, we left that field and on our way back to the farm buildings we secured a number of chases, picking up a few more rabbits before reaching Steve's van.

The final count for our evening's endeavours was four rabbits each for the two old timers, and one for the youngster. Not a great score, but under the far-from-favourable conditions of the evening, still quite acceptable and an exciting night out nevertheless.

We travelled the hour's journey home with a lot of dog talk and banter filling the air. I really enjoyed that early season outing, and both Steve and I agreed we should do it again.

Lamping is one of the greatest sporting opportunities available for both lurcher and owner. It can be the channel for training the young, for keeping the old fit and active, or the means to provide those possessing the right dog, right land and plenty of rabbits, the chance to account for exceptionally large hauls.

But, as we established on this particular night of social lamping, it takes many things to have a good night out. Catching rabbits is just one of them.

CHAPTER II

EYES DOWN FOR A NIGHT'S LAMPING

One week after securing our largest ever haul of rabbits in one night's lamping with lurchers, the Scottish Borders beckoned again. The winds that I constantly prayed for swept through the bars of the dog runs. My lurchers were restless and on edge, as if they could hear the ghosts of their ancestors howling through the mists of time telling them another hunt was near.

In the 1500s, this Scottish border country where most of my hunting takes place, was controlled almost completely by the powerful Armstrong family. So influential was this clan, that a concerned King James V invited John Armstrong to meet him at Hawick and promptly hanged him. The family, however, got their own back when they refused to support King James in the invasion of England and in the Battle of Solway Moss in 1542, where the King lost his life. The Armstrong family motto also remains quite fitting to these wild lands: *Invictus maneo*, which means 'I remain unvanquished'.

This unconquered, hostile environment is approximately 75 miles from my Northumberland home, and the hunting in this Anglo-Scottish border setting certainly doesn't suit all lurcher composites, or indeed their owners. The terrain is hilly and the soil is filled with sharp stone and flint. Dogs required to hunt efficiently here must be full of stamina, tough, durable, agile and possess the temperament to chase large numbers of game over a long shift.

There are vast rabbit populations to be found here, but they still have to be chased and caught. They don't, as novices or ill-informed individuals would have us believe, give themselves up and jump into the hunter's game bag. It takes a special breed of dog to regularly hunt here and be successful, consistently taking numbers between 30 and 80 rabbits per night. Dogs from various parts of Great Britain, and some pure breeds that are good workers in their own right, won't automatically make the grade on this stage.

I have heard boasts by lurchermen of how diminutive whippet composites missed nothing in their own environments, but in this border country I have seen dogs of this breeding that literally had to be carried back to the car. Collie crosses are seen by a fair number of hunters as being good all-rounders but I've seen many sickened to the point of standstill. Various saluki hybrids that have accompanied us, although being stamina-packed, rarely possess what was required mentally to do a full shift when we tried them on ground they obviously didn't appreciate.

Numerous reports in farming and sporting publications or in MAFF literature during 1996 of rabbits reaching plague proportions in Scotland were more or less correct. I have hunted many areas of this beautiful country for over 25 years, during which time I have regularly found individual farms to have rabbit numbers that were higher than normal. One 1500-acre hill-farm I secured for my sport during my semi-professional, vermin-controlling days had such a problem. This may have been great for me as a hunter, but it was a dilemma and major problem for the landowner who was suffering financially. So it will be no surprise that it was this farm that we would be visiting again for this particular nocturnal outing.

I remember well, the afternoon when I first met the land-owner, Jim Sutherland, and how my natural scepticism led me to doubt his claims of securing in excess of 10,000 rabbits a year. However, after we obtained this farm, the rabbit capital of the Scottish Borders, we caught over 3,000 rabbits between the months of August and December, thus making the landowner's claims that much more credible.

Later, as we began to win the battle to gain this farmer's trust, we also assisted with setting and emptying 100 or so wire, catch-alive traps for him. The chap who delivered them that first day told us the best item to entice the rabbits into the trap was carrot. He also advised that it would probably take up to a week before the rabbits got used to these alien contraptions that had invaded their space and began to enter them.

The next day I received a telephone call. 'Better come up today, Bill, if you can.' When we arrived, every trap held a rabbit; on some, buzzards sat with their heads cocked to one side, eyeing up the contents. So much for letting traps weather.

These traps did become yet another weapon in the landowner's arsenal against his rabbit invaders, but for us lamping with dogs would always be the chief activity.

We travelled north like the historical southern nobles and gentlemen who hunted the thieves of Annerdaill and Liddis-daill, and who took with them good dogs to hunt deer and hare on their campaigns. We also took good dogs with us. However, our quest was not to seize vagabonds, but to help rid the land from the scourge of the destructive rabbit.

The physical attributes of my strain of lurchers make them not only a joy to own, but also trusted hunting allies. My dogs were originally bred from working deer-

Sophie, a 5th generation lurcher × lurcher

hounds mated to sound greyhounds. Then over many years the size was 'bred down', mainly by keeping the smallest, keenest bitch from each generation.

I always prefer smaller lurchers for all-round hunting, but not too small. An Arab thoroughbred horse is swift and agile. It is also small, intelligent and extremely strong. It possesses incredible endurance without being coarse or cloddy. These are the virtues I seek in all my dogs, lurchers and deerhounds.

The leash of lurchers on this outing was a family affair: Yella and two of her daughters, Sophie and Jade. Yella and Sophie were two of three dogs that took 213 rabbits in one night, and a week earlier 80 and 81 rabbits, respectively, on these same grounds. On that evening Sophie also caught two hares.

On our arrival, we found the higher, more productive area of the farm thick with mist. The lower ground, however, still provided us with unlimited sport. In the first field, Kevin, Sophie's owner, and I split up. I worked the left side and Kevin ran his dog to the right. The third member of our team, Jason, took his lurcher, Jade, over the hill to the other side of the farm. This was to make sure we covered the whole area and didn't get in each other's way.

The catching started almost immediately. I took the first five rabbits out of five races with Yella. By the sounds emanating from my right, I gathered Kevin was also achieving good results with his bitch. At one point, I was awkwardly carrying a number of rabbits in my hand and going on to the next for Yella to chase. The only breather for my old girl was when cramp in my hand caused me to pause and couple the rabbits to my carrying belt. Once these were securely fastened, I stood up, switched on my lamp and we were on our way once again, the eager lurcher showing no signs whatsoever of wanting to stop.

The fence at the far side of the field seemed to take forever to reach. When I eventually did arrive, I flashed my lamp as a signal to my hunting companion, who was still notching up rabbits with Sophie. He flashed back and began to make his way slowly towards me. I removed the mass of rabbits from my belt and counted them, 20 in total. I knew there was quite a few as I was nearly at the point of beginning to struggle.

At a show, I once explained to a lurcher lad how a friend and I killed over 90 rabbits on grounds well off the beaten track, and how we spent more time ferrying the haul to the roadside, than actually killing them.

'You should have carried 40-odd each and it would

have meant just one trip,' he relied from his less than expert perspective. This is one example of how to catch folk out, how to sort the wheat from the chaff, the talkers from the walkers, the lads who know the crack from those who haven't got a clue what they're talking about. I've heard some lurchermen, apparent supermen, boasting of carrying such numbers. But this is bunkum, pure bunkum. I have carried over 20 on many, many occasions, and believe you me they are a very heavy weight. Along with a battery, this is a load too much for most individuals to carry. Even if the caught rabbits are gutted, the weight difference is hardly noticeable.

As Kevin staggered up, he resembled 'Cousin It' from the Adams family. Rabbits were hanging from him everywhere. He went down on his knees, nigh on incapacitated with the sheer weight, and began to remove his catch.

'Christ, Bill,' he said, with a proud laugh. 'Haven't got a clue how many I've got here, but I'm fucking knackered.'

'Yella's got 20,' I replied, rubbing my aching shoulder as I separated the rabbits he was throwing on the grass.

He, or should I say Sophie, had also taken 20 rabbits from this first field. If Jason had caught a similar amount over the other side of the hill, we would have already notched up a very healthy number.

We placed our combined catch in lines next to the fence, their white bellies pointing skywards, I have always been a great believer in the proper handling of game: I hate to see rabbits just dumped in a heap, or have them squashed in deep, plastic carrying bags. We then proceeded the short distance to the next stage of our outing.

Again we split up, this time in a field in some ways different to the first. Instead of longish grass, this field was the first step of much steeper land. The grass itself was short-cropped, but it possessed many clumps of spiny, longer grass and numerous thistle beds. A quick scan with my lamp revealed one hell of a lot of rabbits, some moving, others clamped close to the ground, taking advantage of the lush vegetation.

In this situation, as a profit hunter, I always make for the rabbits that could be classed as 'easier', those squatting or moving close at hand being the first choice. We were here to do a job for the landowner as well as securing a large tally of rabbits to sell, so numbers were the order of the night. One for the pot, long slipping or going home after a certain number were all out of bounds.

I strode towards a large group of rabbits a fair distance from their safe homes on the other side of the fence line. Yella was on the lead at this point but she was pulling and itching to get going. Yella is an experienced campaigner and looks down the beam of light as soon as its long finger points into the darkness, so she like me could make out the rabbits running and sitting tight.

As a taker of rabbits, Yella is one of the best I've owned and, because of this, she does take a good percentage of the ones she chases. Her main hunting trait is to stalk out slowly, then with a few yards to go she quickens her pace and makes a dart. She either picks the rabbit up in its seat or within a few yards of the creature lifting, both of which are acceptable when a long night's hunting is expected. I have also seen her anticipating which way the rabbit is going to lift and she dives to one side to pick it up. This looks great when it comes off, but comical when the dog goes one way and the rabbit the other.

On this sloping ground, Yella caught her first three rabbits squatting. The rest were runners, a combination of both short and longish runs. It's helpful when a dog obtains squatters or rabbits that don't give them too much trouble, but it doesn't always work that way. My bitch, however, was really striking well, and I was expecting another record-breaking haul at this point.

Again I was positioned where I could hear, and at times see, Kevin lamping – what a great little bitch Sophie is! Yella's wagging tail also showed her approval of her daughter's rabbit-taking ability.

Up and up we headed, until the land levelled off and we finally met up at an old wooden, lichen-covered gate in the top corner of this rough grazing. Both of us had again achieved double figures, but these rabbits had been

Kevin and Sophie, with one of her many double figured hauls of rabbits

noticeably more difficult than those taken early on.

Following the customary sorting out, we sat and rested for a while, watching the occasional shaft of light from Jason's lamp waving across the star-filled sky. Suddenly we were enveloped in a cloud of dampness that pierced our flesh and touched our bones, as fog slowly descended like a grey spectre. This was to drive us back down, but we thought if we were quick we could still kill a few more rabbits on our descent.

Fog here comes in at an alarming pace; it is quite dangerous as it disorientates even those who know the terrain well. When lamping you must expect bad weather from time to time. Rain, although wet, does seem to assist, as does wind obviously. But fog helps no one: it is an enemy of man and beast. Once its blanket is laid, winds usually subside, plunging the land into a stillness that allows every creature to detect your approach easily and so make for safety. The lamp becomes useless as the once penetrating beam ricochets off a wall of fog.

On the way down, the dogs did take a number of rabbits as we made for our spoils cooling at the edge of the first field. It would have been nigh on impossible to carry the lot, so we decided to let the dogs run free so that the rabbits could be coupled to the dog-leaders. The haul was then dragged behind us over grass that had been lightly washed by the descending fog and was exceedingly slippery.

We met up with Jason in the darkness as we were ferrying our catch to the roadside. Jason's bitch wasn't as experienced a lamper as my dogs or Kevin's, and was fairly new to the lamping for numbers game. Her greenness on this occasion saw her catch only six rabbits, but at this point it was her personal best, and Jason was more than happy. Yella took a bag of 42, and Kevin's bitch 46, a good overall tally with which we were extremely pleased.

As we gutted the rabbits and fed the offal to the crystal clear waters of a fast flowing burn where such nutrient rich deposits were useful, the weather turned really bad. The fog had stalked us down to the lower ground, and to add to our discomfort the heavens opened their floodgates and we were deluged by a downpour.

We loaded up our vehicle, changed into warmer, dryer clothes and set off south for our long journey home. The evening's exploits were a good topic of conversation as our vehicle gobbled up the 100 or so miles back to England.

The excitement of that night stayed with me and, during the next few days, it spurred me on to recharge my battery and to prepare the dogs for their next stiff test, two nights later.

It is work like this that helps maintain good strains of lurchers to a high standard, consistently performing well and taking large numbers of rabbits on any terrain. These are traits which dogs from my kennel and some individual dogs of selected hunting friends possess in abundance.

CHAPTER 12

THE NORTH WIND DOTH BLOW

During the latter part of 2002, we endured hard winter weather that left the rugged landscape of my beautiful Northumberland shrouded in a deep blanket of snow. Snow-covered fields meant new opportunities for my dog pack and me: detective work in the local countryside I arrogantly believe I know so well.

For the shy inhabitants of the area, these white weather conditions are just another danger sent to weed out the weak. It is mother nature's way of ensuring only the strong survive to propagate the various species.

Amid this wildlife-rich landscape, adjacent to my Ashington home, lies the reclaimed industrial land that was once a thriving mining area, where buckets of coal hung from cables like a murky necklace across the skyline. Soaring shale heaps were spread across the county like gigantic mole hills, and rusty burns sneaked through the course of hedgerows on their journey via the river Wansbeck to the grey North Sea. Nowadays these lands are somewhat rejuvenated, rising from the white-hot ashes of their industrial heritage. Trees now dress what is left of the man-made heaps, reduced in size through the extraction of red shale to form the base of many local motorways, roads and factories. Flora and fauna thrive on what was once desolate mud flats and pit dumping grounds.

Throughout every season of the year I find solitude when walking here. The fox, hare and rabbit that sometimes share time with me on my visits have all learned that men with

Snow-covered rigs

dogs mean trouble. When I am lucky enough to observe any of this trio, they quickly disappear into the surroundings, leaving me wondering, 'Where did it go?'

Securing a rabbit or hare for the pot with a dog on a stage where they are chased one way or another every day and night of their lives, requires a dog possessing more than just good eyesight. A finely-honed scenting ability is just as important, if not more so. Such dogs have the ability to catch the scent of a hare carried on the iciest wind or the odour of a rabbit over the barest ground of exposed shale.

Quarry species now living among the newly-planted fir trees or on the rough, grassy embankments rarely show themselves. They nervously venture out from their hidden retreats early in the morning or at dusk. However the advent of snow can lend us a helping hand to observe or hunt them, as footprints and tracks leave behind a record of their wanderings.

Between Christmas and the New Year, I ventured out for a stroll through what the locals call 'over the back' with my trusted companions, a lurcher and deerhound. The sapling fir trees were well dusted with a powdery covering of snow, maintaining that Christmassy feeling of a few days before. I was well wrapped up in presents of a hand-knitted Arran jumper, a knitted pom-pom hat and new Hunter Wellingtons thirsting for a muddy pool to dive into.

My outing took me along hedges of thick hawthorn, hacked down to a handy height ideal for greenfinches and scribbly-Jacks (yellow-hammers) to nest in during spring and summer. Along the border of this grassland lay a bewildering pattern of tracks and scratchings, mainly left by rabbits playing in snow, a phenomenon that some of them had never seen before. The tracks were deep, but little or no smell remained to over-excite the dogs.

My old lurcher, Yella, was first to be spurred into action as she eventually picked up an interesting, fresher trail of scent, and she set off at pace, zigzagging towards a large patch of gorse and tangled, low-lying bramble. Gwen, my deerhound bitch, followed close behind, while I scrutinised the environment closely after seeing the old dog's reaction. Yella quickened her pace to a rate of knots and her tail pointed stiffly towards the grey, snow-filled sky, leading me to believe her target wasn't too far away.

Sure enough, a flash of brown fur suddenly split from the shadowy undergrowth, exploding from the prickly gorse about a yard in front of my old dog's nose. She lunged into action, with speed reminiscent of when she could still give a fit brown hare a run for its money. The deerhound, observing the commotion from its position within the gorse, loped over the prickly barrier and also made off in hot pursuit.

Only bursts of the ensuing chase could be seen from the track where I was positioned. The determination of my lurcher pressed the rabbit to break out onto more open ground.

133

Once again I had the pleasure of watching a lurcher that had passed every test set her. No plodding with this old girl. No half-heartedness either and no second chances given to a fleeing rabbit that could have made a lesser dog look silly. A lightening strike ended the contest in a spray of fine snow.

Yella retrieved her prey with Gwen attempting to steel the rabbit from her clenched jaws. The deerhound would have to wait for the lurcher to drop this one to get it from her, and that wasn't likely to happen! The limp body of the already dead rabbit was duly put into the safety of the deep inside pocket of my coat. We trekked off once again, hoping this time to find the tracks of a more formidable adversary, in the form of a brown hare, to match the quality of my team.

We moved on to more open ground. Here I observed an assortment of tracks and footprints preserved in the snow. Rodent tracks, characterised by their small size and the four widely-spreading toes of their front feet, were almost every-where. I hadn't realised till then how many wood mice, pigmy and common shrew there are residing here. I had, however, observed many short-eared owls over the summer months. I now know why! The success of these silent, broad-winged spectres depends on the food sources available to them.

Yella and Gwen checking scents in the snow

The mustalid family also left many tell-tale signs for me to puzzle over. It is not only important to know the shape and size of animal prints, but also to be aware of the creatures' movements. Weasels and stoats tend to jump, land, then take off again from the same spot. Their larger relative, the badger, also produces this pattern when bounding, but when walking they leave a slightly staggered evenly spaced line of tracks.

As I meandered along, following and inspecting every possible track, I found that a fox had also toured the area recently, scavenging for his breakfast and at the same time leaving his prints about a yard out from the hedge. Foxes, when travelling, leave a line of paired prints, where both front and back feet are placed in the same hole. The distance between these prints can give an indication of whether the animal was walking, trotting or running.

Common tracks tend to become familiar, so more attention is generally paid to the unusual. Last year, I remember following a set of strange marks. These turned out to be a hare with both its back legs caught up in a wire snare, the device having being pulled from its securing point by a creature it probably wasn't intended to take.

More recognisable hare tracks on this occasion were conspicuous only by their absence. I found this strange, as a couple of local lurcher lads told me they had seen a few nervous hares two nights earlier when they were out with the lamp they got from Santa Claus. But this can be a trait of hares: some do tend to wander a lot, while others may live a solitary existence in one or two fields.

Then, lo and behold, the long, baseball-bat shape of a hare's hind legs lay fresh in the soft snow. These tracks were going off in the direction of an area of ridges where young conifers were planted with parade-like straightness. I walked to the peak of one of these channels so I was able to make out the tracks below in the depths of the furrow. The lurcher and deerhound walked one either side.

A family covey of grey partridges that had roosted tail-to-tail in the middle of the field during the night caused a false alarm. They had arrived at these rigs early for safety and to scratch out a meal but were hunted out and lifted thanks to some good nose work by Gwen. The birds took off heavily with rapid wing beats and then glided towards the grey horizon. I watched the group as they glided and landed as one in the next field.

There was no visual sign of the prey we sought. My dogs followed the hare's scent to the edge of a plantation of half-grown fir-trees swaying gently in the breeze, their heads shaking as if telling us not to enter. The dogs ran among the saplings, searching, darting with noses trained to the ground and eyes scanning at the same time for any flash of movement. After a short period both dogs returned, one following the other, but with the occasional look behind as if they had heard a whisper. Hares on this constantly-hunted terrain tend to learn quickly and move off as soon as men or dogs are detected. It was beginning to look like we would be unsuccessful on this excursion.

I moved up across a number of furrows, walking slowly and making my way back in the direction of the path that would guide us to the fields, then homewards. There was now no sign of tracks whatsoever as I strode through the snow. My dogs followed at heel, aware that my excitement had lessened. I was now just taking in the beautiful scenery and gone were the stirring tone in my voice and the urgency in my pace.

At that point, for some unknown reason, I glanced down and found a set of old prints. The next thing I knew, a full-grown hare burst from the ground in front of me, leaving shrapnel of soil and snow in its wake as it emerged. The creature ran back the way I had just come, right between my two canine companions. The dogs set off in blistering pursuit. I scrambled quickly to the highest vantage point I could find to watch the chase.

My pair darted back and forth over the rigs near the edge of the plantation with total disregard for the dangers of running on this rough, undulating ground. This hare was certainly leading them a merry dance. Hares more often than not have an escape route planned in case of emergency, but with the dogs working this one so well, it was soon making its way back towards me with both dogs hot on its heels. I made a split-second decision about where to position myself, for fear of getting knocked over by two canine missiles locked on to their target.

Closer and closer they came. I could now see the magnificent, russet colours of the hare and behind it, the glaring eyes and bared ivory teeth of the dogs. The creature was nearly on top of me when Yella put in an extra dash in an attempt to end the chase. She missed with her strike by a couple of inches. I heard the clap of her jaws as she struck. The hare would have felt the dog's hot breath on its back. This near miss also made the hare turn back on itself. With the deerhound just five yards behind and homing in, this was to be a serious miscalculation.

Gwen struck at the hare and she too just missed as the creature cleverly jinked at the last moment. Yella by now had recovered and again she took over the course. The hare just couldn't shake her off. Then the lurcher tried again and this time made no mistake in striking her target. What an incredible spectacle I was fortunate enough to have witnessed, a chase that any number of superlatives would still fail to describe.

I sat on a cold seat with the still warm, but lifeless hare lying by my side. What beautiful animals hares are. This was an adult female, in exceptional condition with a full, thick winter coat. The dogs were also paying great attention to their adversary. They stood in the snow with steam rising from their bodies and their tongues hanging so far out they nearly reached the ground. All the natural sounds of this setting were for the moment covered by the panting of the weary dogs. I spoke to both with a great deal of praise, and they crawled on their bellies in the snow towards me. I was now in no hurry. I had obtained far more than I could ever have hoped for, so I allowed the dogs plenty of time to recover.

Eventually, I got up to set off home and caught sight of another hare slinking over the ridges in the distance, far too long a slip on this ground. Enough was enough for today, I thought, and distracted the dogs so they wouldn't see it. That one will do for another day either as an exerciser or, like the one in my hand, for the pressure cooker.

The snow had held off during the course but now, the demonstration over, it began to fall thick and fast. We battled our way through the blizzard, to the warmth of a fireside for me and to a bed of sweet, dry straw for my two girls.

This winter's harsh weather had afforded me great pleasure, ensuring unforgettable memories that would stay with me forever. An added blessing was that my two dogs got fitter and gained experience and at the same time provided me with a rabbit for a pie, a hare for my freezer and a great day out following animal tracks in the snow.

CHAPTER 13
EARLY SUCCESS

A year had passed since my lurcher bitch, Yella, was mated. The aim of the union was to continue my line of lurchers started in the 70s. The carefully chosen mate for Yella was one of her full grandsons, and five fit and healthy pups resulted: three bitches and two dogs.

Two of the progeny, one male and one female, showed the most unusual coat coloration of black and tan. Some friends in the lurcher world, not aware of Yella's ancestry, were astounded. I, on the other hand, was well aware of the origins of such colouring: through the genes of a black-and-tan, gypsy-bred dog named Paddy.

Paddy was the son of a bob-tailed, collie-cross bitch called Sheba, nick named 'the Dulux bitch'. This lurcher was noted for her incredible intelligence and guile when running on the back of a hare. Shortly after arriving at her new home in Ashington, she mysteriously disappeared. A vigilante assemblage of lurcher enthusiasts took it upon themselves to pay a friendly visit to the Hartford gypsy camp, and the true owner eventually recovered the bitch from swarthy-faced individuals reluctant to hand her over.

Paddy's sire was a dog called Snatch, and although this animal was a useful worker in the field and always accounted for his fair share of hares, fox and deer over a season, he became a sheep dog. He was not like the clever border collies that starred in Phil Drabble's *One Man and His Dog*, but instead was one of those hands-over-the-face dogs that farmers shoot on sight for ripping the throats out of their stock. Snatch also

Mother and daughter, Yella and Pup

caused a number of his owners to end up with black eyes and broken noses as he was passed down the line, his fault masked during any sale or transaction. Rumour has it that he was eventually taken over the local fields, tethered to a fence post and shot. Sheep killers, dogs that quit and those prone to injuries were not tolerated in those days.

Paddy never emulated his father's most hideous of crimes. He was as biddable around sheep as he was ruthless with foxes. As an all-round hunter he was undoubtedly one of the best male lurchers in Northumberland during this era. For many years he held the local record for the number of hares taken during an evening's work. Yes, his owner lamped hares, as did everyone with a dog at that time, but at least Paddy could also take this quarry during the daytime. He was one of only a handful of local, male lurchers that genuinely took over 100 hares in his life. He was also a formidable taker of roe deer.

On one occasion when digging a fox out of a 'one-holer' at the Barrington refuse tip near Bedlington, the fox was holed up in a stop, spitting and snarling at the terriers working him. We pulled the terriers back; Paddy latched on to the fox's head and drew him out in one powerful pull. The pair was locked jaw to jaw. The fox bit hard but this only made the dog grip tighter. Paddy went into a frenzy and killed this fox without any assistance. At this time of my life, I was a practicing taxidermist. I mounted this fox's mask for Paddy's owner, but not before doing a lot of remedial work on the jaws and skull with apoxy resins, brass pins and plaster of Paris bandages.

Paddy was not what I would call the fastest lurcher I have witnessed; in fact his owner would often stand, open-mouthed, watching the speed and tightness of turning of my bitch Bes, and later her daughter Kit. Paddy's greatest attributes were his hunting temperament, striking ability and tremendous stamina.

I hunted with Paddy as part of my team for many seasons. I was also there on the night his lamping career, and his life, ended. I watched excitedly as the dog jumped over a fence after a rabbit but as he picked up his prey he struck an overturned sheep trough. He returned with the rabbit in his jaws, but his leg swung like a pendulum as he cleared the barbs of the fence's top wire. His distraught owner guided me over to him with his flashlight.

'Dok, I think he's broke his leg,' he said to me, his voice shaking and full of anxiety. I checked the dog's leg, which was now fully articulated, moveable in every direction.

'You think it's broke – it's a knacker-job, Billy,' I told him. Tears immediately filled his eyes, and I must admit I couldn't offer him any more advice due to a lump in my own throat that was the size of an orange.

His leg was completely shattered and that dog never uttered a murmur. He jumped into the back of the Diahatsu Fourtrak unaided. I coupled his back legs together for support; still not a squeak. We got bogged down before we got out of the field; Paddy just lay there quite unperturbed as we dug the vehicle out. It is instances like this that remind me why I picked this dog out as a sire to my pups. His memory and his progeny remain as his legacy, to Billy and me, and to the local lurcher population in the years that followed, a sporting era when proper lurchers like Paddy ruled the roost.

Of all the male lurchers I knew of, it was Paddy that impressed me the most, and because of this I mated him to my own bitch, Bes, a bitch I always consider to have been my best all-rounder.

Bes was extremely fast and fleet of foot. She was often the last dog running on a hard day coursing hares or an exhausting night lamping rabbits. If she had a failing, as every dog does, I never detected it in the 13 grand years I worked her.

This diminutive bitch excelled in securing vast numbers of rabbits at that time and was another of that exclusive band of mid-Northumbrian dogs, along with her new mate, that took over 100 hares. Many people boasted of their dogs taking this magic number, but during the 1980s, even with the advent of lamping, such a quantity was restricted only to the best. Bes also caught many roe deer and foxes. Birds were another speciality of this bitch, and her ornithological catches included red grouse, partridge, pheasant, a couple of ducks, a skylark and my wife's pet budgerigar.

The pairing of these two exceptional running dogs produced, as expected, some wonderful all-round hunters. Dogs of this quality deserve to be in the hands of true hunting enthusiasts. Unfortunately, some of the men who obtained pups from me were not as dedicated as they led me to believe: part-timers who would never get the dogs to realise their full potential. Lurchers akin to these need graft, not just one or two excursions a month. They were designer dogs, aimed at the profit-hunter market of enthusiastic dog men and people who walked the fields as opposed to just talking about it.

John 'Ginger' Alderton and Silk

My bitch, Yella, was a product of two generations further down the line, after another injection of blood from useful, local dogs. So from the brief history of her breeding that I have given, it will be no surprise why I retained the black-and-tan rough-coated bitch for myself out of the litter. Her similar-coloured, but smooth-haired sibling made the long journey to Exmoor, to a good friend, Jim Vickers, who was involved with a hunt there, a man who knew my breed and its attributes well.

'Pup', as the bitch I kept was named, was Paddy reincarnated, albeit in miniature form. It was the beginning of August when I decided she was ready for her initiation into work. So fellow lurcher enthusiast, John Alderton, and I organised a night out hunting rabbits. Our outing took place on land within earshot of the North Sea's thunderous roar.

Ginger's lurcher dog, Silk, was a relatively experienced lamper of rabbits, he possessed a fair amount of saluki in his breeding, which manifested itself much in the dog's appearance. I have always found that these saluki crosses, although stamina-packed, regularly lack the temperament required to chase rabbit after rabbit on the lamp. I must admit they have never done anything for me. If I lived on or near the Fens, it might have been another story.

Even though Ginger's dog had never been truly tested on large numbers of rabbits, as commonly found a little further north on the Scottish Borders, he had worked the awkward ground of this particular farm many times. The ground here was a mixture of lush fields, rough grazing and awkward sand dunes.

A large percentage of chases here see the dog obtaining only brief glimpses of the fleeing rabbits, so they must be forever alert and possess a keen, well-trained eye. Success at times relies not so much on what the dog can keep sight of, but more on its ability to home in on the noise of the rabbit as the creature passes quickly through varying lengths of sea-grass, temporarily vanishing from sight. In this situation a great majority of dogs will return empty-handed. Not ours! The hunting prowess of the lurchers we own and work has rarely left us wallowing in failure.

Knowing what is required here, however, I experienced a small degree of doubt about whether my sapling would secure her first kill on the dunes on her very first visit. I wondered whether a more suitable terrain for her age might have been a better plan. Maybe the bordering grass fields might suit her inexperience better, so to begin the night's sport we followed a track that meandered along the edge of the fearsome dunes in the direction of a five-bar gate and the entrance to inviting sleeping grass fields.

As we made our way slowly, the beam from Ginger's lamp flashed back and forth in front of us. Our eyes were now accustomed to the darkness and so focused on the grass, scanning for any movement. It wasn't long before a suitable rabbit was spotted. Ginger is never one to wait around to find out what a rabbit is going to do, or whose turn it is for a race, and Silk was released.

Good lamping dogs should at least follow the beam of light even if they have not pin-pointed the exact position of the rabbit when slipped. This is what Silk proceeded to do on this occasion. Suddenly the rabbit lifted, the dog spotted it and the chase was on. Although the run was in full view of us, Pup had her nose fixed to a scent on the ground. She missed most of the good chase and the pick-up by Ginger's dog.

Silk chased another rabbit but Pup once again learnt very little from it. Then the chance I had prayed for. A rabbit was being chased in our direction by Ginger's dog. As it passed I swung around and eagerly slipped my youngster. Off she ran in hot pursuit, quickly catching up the impressive, running Silk. As she drew level, Silk snapped the rabbit up in full flight. He got the rabbit but Pup, more importantly for me, had obtained her first chase and witnessed, if not felt, the excitement of a rabbit being caught.

The next couple of races saw my novice lurcher standing on her hind legs observing the spectacle. That first race had really done the trick to ignite the flame of interest; her keenness was now such that I decided it was time for her to have a run on her own, or risk her 'opening up', barking with excitement.

A quick scan into the fields with my lamp revealed a number of rabbits already on the move. I could sense Ginger's itchy fingers wanting to slip his dog. I made for one of the rabbits furthest from the fence, but then I caught the ruby eyes of another squatting, glinting in the spread of my lamp. This was a lot closer, so I led Pup to it.

The ears of the edgy creature lifted, a sure sign it was getting nervous and about to lift. As it did, Pup lunged forward. Obviously she had seen it, so with no hesitation I released her. She ran straight onto the trail of the rabbit. Her prey jinked as it ran, attempting to outwit the dog, but Pup stuck to her task well, matching every scurrying movement. As the chasing pair swung around they were now making towards the fence. The rabbit made it to the barrier, going through it without missing a beat although I had flashed my light off in an attempt to disorientate it. This obstruction didn't put Pup off in the least: with an echoing twang she also went through, losing tufts of hair from her back as she did so. Once out of the field she went out of my beam, disappearing into the shadows of the adjacent sand dunes. Ginger however was in a spot to take over at this point, keeping the rabbit in the hot spot of his beam for my pup to follow. As I ran to the fence, my friend's light danced a merry jig over the small hills and hollows. The beam then stopped in one position, coinciding with the noise that told me the rabbit was caught, but which dog had got it? Had Pup been successful, or did Ginger slip his dog? A moment later and my youngster emerged from the herb-rich dune slacks, proud as punch, with a rabbit locked in her jaws. 'Over the moon' is an understatement of how I felt. Young lurchers can be a right old headache at times, but when they obtain their first kill, annoyance, frustration and disappointments are all forgotten for a time. It is a time to party.

When I met up with Ginger, he told me how the rabbit could not shake off my dog. 'She is a very tight little bitch, Dok, like a bloody hoover,' he said excitedly.

It was dark and the salt-tasting, stiff breeze blew into our faces as we sat for a time, letting the land settle before re-entering the grassy field. Then, once again, the lamps were illuminated. The resident rabbits looked undisturbed, going about their business as normal. I now had the confidence to give Pup another run and the youngster sensed my intention. The field was large; Ginger and I decided to split up and go in different directions.

The next chase for my lurcher was a rabbit not too far away, cutting right across my path as it headed for the sanctuary of the dunes. A number of the rabbits here seem to be aware of the dangers of the lamp and we saw them making a similar run for safety. This was the first that was close enough to be of any use. My bitch had seen it, so I slipped her as the rabbit crossed a sandy ride used by the farmer to train his racehorses. As I released her, I momentarily thought I had been a bit rash. I thought this one was away, but then it came back through the fence into the field as if it had forgotten something.

Pup took full advantage of this mistake and chased the rabbit like an old campaigner. Once again showing how tight she is as she jinked and twisted behind the bobbing creature. To end the contest she made what I can only describe as a breathtaking strike. She is truly Paddy's daughter I thought to myself. Again, she returned the spoils to my waiting hand.

After a few more unsuccessful races, two rabbits was to be her final tally for the night. Such an achievement may seem mediocre, but it was double what I hoped for before the evening started. Ginger's dog, Silk, took eight rabbits, giving us a nice round number for the outing.

When bringing on young lurchers, it is all too easy to get carried away and slip the saplings on rabbit after rabbit. Lamping must be presented as a game during those early outings otherwise continually missing rabbits quickly becomes a chore and an exhausting one at that. Pup was looking for more, but her enthusiasm would keep for another evening. Lamping for this bitch would remain an entertainment to her and one she would be only too eager to take part in again. There was no hurry.

This little bitch had much to do to emulate some of the excellent dogs in her ancestry, lurchers long since gone to that big coursing ground in the sky but which will be observing from another plane how she fares in the coming weeks, months and years. Just because her phenotype resembles that of Paddy doesn't guarantee she will possess his outstanding ability. But at least now she is off the mark as a taker of coney.

Politics permitting, she definitely has the pedigree to follow her ancestors as one of the county's elite in the secretive world of hunting with the lamp. If this first showing is anything to go by, she may also possess the ability!

CHAPTER 14

SOMETHING COMPLETELY DIFFERENT

'How's that pup coming on?' asked one of the local lurcher lads, passing me as I walked with the
youngster through the main street of Ashington.

'Oh, quite well,' I answered. 'She's had her first kill
and she's coming along nicely, very nicely, and—'

I never finished the rest of my sentence, apprehen-
sion blocking out further speech. I didn't want to say
too much about her progress or be forced to listen to
a long-winded, exaggerated boast of one of his pups
catching its first hare at five months of age, securing
100 rabbits on the lamp at six months and pulling down
its first deer at nine months. So I bantered for a short
while, politely bid my farewell and left.

I was more than happy with the youngster's progress
and the moon had waxed and waned since the evening
when 'Pup' caught her first rabbit. I call her Pup not as
an insult or from any lack of imagination on my part
but simply because the name stuck when I picked out
this particular pup from the litter I had bred.

The genotype of this youngster dictates she will be
far more than just a rabbit dog. Although the taking
of rabbits by day and by night will constitute a fairly
large proportion of her working career, hares too will be
a legitimate quarry for her. She is bred from great all-
rounders, not one-quarry wonders.

Although early success on rabbits has always been
one of the main components in the bringing on of my

149

young running dogs, I never set an age for a dog's initiation with hares. All dogs are individuals and must be treated as such, and experience has taught me the folly of entering a running dog too early against such an athlete as the brown hare. Rabbits or blue hares are a different story as these can be ideal competition for a lurcher just learning its trade. But brown hares? Well, these are creatures to be worked up to gradually.

My youngster's mother, Yella, accounted for her first hare when she was 13 months old. At the same age she had caught a total of 512 rabbits. Her great grandmother, Bes, killed her first hare when she was six months, but it was another four months before she caught her second. At a year old, Bes had taken over 100 rabbits. She also had a number of fox and a roe deer to her credit. I have highlighted these differentials to show how dogs enter on hare at different ages. The rule of thumb is 'never be in too much of a hurry'.

Two of the previously mentioned lurchers, Bes and Yella, were produced from lurcher × lurcher matings, using dogs with a fair amount of deerhound in their genetic make up. This is a type within the lurcher breed that I have specialised in over a long period of time. My enthusiasm in my younger days was such that I ventured out into the countryside more than most other lurcher buffs, so a specialist dog in the form of the all-rounder has always been my type of dog.

During my involvement with running dogs, no other type of lurcher has been able to offer what I need from a worker. I intentionally set my standards high – better too high than too low. Some lurchers, especially those from first-cross matings, need a little longer to mature mentally and physically before entering. The adaptable all-round lurcher has to be held back at times.

Over a long period of time I have also been involved in producing F1 deerhound × greyhounds but my strain of working lurchers could knock the spots off any individual of this cross for all-round ability.

The deerhound × greyhounds, although very attractive longdogs, are one of the main crosses which tend to take a little longer to come on. When they are fully developed and set, however, they do make extremely useful killers of hares and, as I often reflect, are probably the most versatile of all the first-cross hybrids. This tendency to enter into work later than other dogs doesn't necessarily make any difference to their final ability. Indeed, over the decades I have found in numerous cases where the slower developing pup in a litter can turn out to be the best worker in the long term.

Mother nature, that skilled creator, fashions animals and their bodies to suit their habits and environments. She has been particularly generous to the lurcher breed on the whole, blessing them with a diversity gifted to no other breed. Pup had already taken one quarry species, and it was time to show what versatility of hunting skill she possessed. Her next step up the hunting ladder would be to pit her against the brown hare.

It was mid-October when I was fortunate enough to acquire another farm on which to work my dogs. A lot of permissions can come quite by accident, from the most unlikely of places or simply through being in the right place at the right time. At this time I was employed by a bus company in rural Northumberland. Although primarily working as an engineer, an element of my occupation was driving. I picked up farmers' kids and took them to schools in Morpeth, Ponteland, Corbridge and Hexham. I really liked the look of one farm I visited in this capacity. It simply oozed wildlife in every shape and form. You just sense certain terrain will house game, and this land screamed at me, 'I have a secret!'

'Are there any rabbits on your farm,' I asked one of the kids who got onto my bus and who I was getting to know fairly well by now.

'There are lots,' he excitedly replied.

'Ask your dad if there's any chance of me coming up to get some with my dogs and ferrets.'

'OK, I'll let you know.'

My forwardness was quite forgotten until a few weeks later: the lad got on my bus and told me his dad said I had to go up and meet him. This I did the following Saturday afternoon, dressed smartly to impress in moleskin trousers, shirt, tie and Tricker brogues – and that was that: more land secured on which to work my dogs.

This farm, as with most others at my disposal, is situated in the north of Northumberland. This is land of which I never tire on my customary journeys of exploration and where everything living there breeds and grows at least a month behind similar flora and fauna just 30 miles south. The terrain is made up mainly of very rough grazing where silage always does better than corn or oil seed rape.

My enthusiasm at obtaining permission to work my dogs over this land meant I was excited and eager to get started straight away, so I planned an excursion a week after meeting the friendly and most accommodating landowner. Accompanying me on this jaunt was Ivor Dixon, a friend and fellow lurcherman of long standing from my hometown of Ashington. Ivor took along his saluki-blooded lurcher, Pip, a dog a little older and more experienced than my own. Although these crosses are somewhat alien to the area and kept more by people keen enough to travel to the Fens to get the best from them, some enthusiasts do try to emulate local dogs that have passed the tests and do the business.

This outing had two main functions: firstly to get us acquainted with the terrain and its boundaries, and secondly to obtain some sport for the two relatively young dogs. We expected rabbits to be the main quarry, but lamping is unpredictable and we were in for a major surprise.

As we entered the first field, shy rabbits slunk away on their bellies, making for the sanctuary of a fence and the plantation it so conscientiously guarded. Ivor, eager as ever, slipped his dog on one of these cagey characters. Pip is not built for speed from a standing start and, as I would have expected, returned empty-mouthed. As Ivor was fastening the slip leader around the slender neck of his dog, I scanned with my lamp in readiness for the next chase. To my surprise, two hares sat feeding towards the middle of the field where my lamp's beam tailed off. We set off cautiously towards them, dogs tethered and ready for action, one lamp illuminating our direct path.

At our initial meeting, the farmer mentioned only ever seeing a small number of these unsociable creatures on his land in the past, but these sightings were on his travels during the day. He did tell me, however, that I could exercise any I came across, but he didn't want them wiped out. Exercise was all we did on these two. We set the more experienced dog away just as the hares started to move on. The lift was long and the distance to the far plantation was small. The hare the dog singled out eventually made its escape after a relatively short chase. Pup watched the spectacle with eager eyes, taking in what she saw and locking it in her intelligent head for future reference.

We progressed slowly back towards the fence line and, at its bare edge, where thousands of sheep had travelled before us, we reached a wooden, five-bar gate that reeked of creosote-based, wood preserver. As we quietly opened it and entered the next meadow, I immediately lit up the field with my lamp before re-closing the gate. I scanned to my right to find a hare already on the move, running up the edge of the pig-mesh fence.

I believed it was my turn and, because of excitement on Ivor's part, we slipped our dogs in unison. The hare's ears were erect, evaluating the situation. As the dogs gained the ears went back, she shifted into another gear and the chase was on. First-cross saluki × greyhounds are rarely noted as speed merchants: most have sacrificed pace for stamina. Pip, however, was a saluki blooded lurcher, and although he isn't fast, these crosses still have a tendency to get stronger as the chase goes on. Ivor's more practised dog did most of the work. Whenever possible, Pup's extra speed challenged defiantly for poll position.

The course lasted what seemed like a lifetime. The hare skilfully dodged between the dogs and lampers. Slowly, the hare worked her way closer and closer to her pre-planned exit. This hare was born in these fields,

154

so she was acquainted with every blade of grass and friendly with each rut and furrow, even in the dark. The dogs stuck to their task well, but this wily creature dived through the fence and to safety after a most entertaining chase.

After a short rest, we prospected once again along the fence, scanning our lamps continuously in order to increase what we could see in the illuminated area. We came upon a terrain where we believed the best plan would be to split up. Ivor was to carry on circumnavigating the field, while my task was to cross a low rolling fell.

On this type of ground I had to pay close attention to where I trod and what was immediately in front of me, as well as to what may be further out, for as was once said, 'The eyes of a fool are in the ends of the earth.' Rabbits squat very tightly and can easily be by-passed, and sure enough within a few hundred yards a crouching rabbit did lift right in front of me. Pup being off her leader at the time ran it well, bowling over and securing her prey very quickly. The youngster caught another couple of rabbits, one from a similar short lift, the second after a lengthier slip. These successes came before she embarked on what would be her stiffest test, not only of the night, but in her lamping career up to that date.

From a distance I spotted what I thought could be a hare squatting. I fastened my dog securely in her slip-lead just in case, as I would have to get as close as I possibly could if she was to stand any chance catching such a beast. As we tentatively approached, I had in the back of my mind what my father always used to say, 'If it gets smaller as you get closer, it's a hare; if it gets bigger, it's a stone or piece of muck.' This object was definitely becoming flatter to the ground on which it lay.

As I neared, I rounded the squatting hare, hoping to drive it to more open ground once it lifted. The creature's reflecting eyes could now be seen. I was now advantageously positioned between fence and hare. Resting hares pick their forms to give both view and shelter, so this individual would not only know our position, but would have an escape route already planned. From experience, I was banking on the fence being its intended exit door.

With only a short distance remaining the hare burst from the grass. My trigger finger clicked the metal quick release, liberating Pup immediately. There was no law given on this run, just a lift of around 20 feet or so: such luxuries and matters of fair play would be kept until this little bitch was a proficient hare taker.

A really good course ensued, with my youngster sticking close to the tail of the hare. The hare tried, but couldn't shake the dog off. I did my part by keeping the two animals in the beam of light. The hare, realising she was starting to loose the race, did what I expected her to do and began to lead the dog straight towards the fence. Hares don't ease up when they use this particular ploy, but neither did Pup.

On the first approach to her way out and freedom, the hare could not commit herself. A turn of nearly 90 degrees took her along the fence, then back into the field. The nippy Pup also spun around tightly, got back onto terms with her prey and once again followed closely behind. A sharp bend saw the pair racing back towards the fence again and this time it would be the hare's downfall. Pup threw herself and took the creature mid-body. Being such a short distance from the fence, my main concern was that Pup wouldn't be able to hold her kicking, thrusting prize possession.

I ran towards the youngster. She was now employing her feet as well as her bite to restrain her catch and I could see there was no way she was going to let this one escape. I grabbed the hare by its long back legs. The fence was just a yard away and I never count anything as caught until it's hanging from my carrying belt. Prising the beast from the dog's jaws I quickly dispatched it: my lurcher's first hare and a single-handed effort to boot.

I know what it is to take many rabbits in a single night with a dog, to witness one of my kennel pull down a roe deer after a lift of half a field and watch as a fox has been caught up with, bowled over and killed. Yet of all the achievements I have experienced with running dogs, there is none which yields so much enjoyment as seeing a pup that I planned, bred and reared accounting for its first hare.

I eagerly caught up with Ivor further up the field, and took great pleasure in showing him my lurcher's good fortune hanging from the strap of my battery pack. Ivor had taken another four rabbits with Pip, but commented that he too had raced a couple of hares and seen many others.

So, at the end of our first evening's outing on this newly acquired land, I knew I had another good farm with permission to work my dogs, not only on rabbits, but on hares too. I also possessed another lurcher that proved it could come to terms successfully and single-handedly on both these quarry species. Pup was a little dog with a big heart that was growing in stature with every outing. She took her hare well, albeit on the lamp at night, although that makes little difference, as in my eyes a hare is a hare is a hare.

CHAPTER 15

IF LOOKS COULD KILL

It has been over 30 years now since a swarthy-faced traveller approached me at the Lowther horse-driving trials near
Penrith in Cumbria.

'Wanna sell yer dog?' he asked in that demanding, tinker-
type tone that can prompt the unsuspecting to contemplate
selling something they would never otherwise consider parting
with. At the same time he looked down, singling out one of the
brace of deerhound-blooded lurchers by my side.

It's strange, isn't it, how something like the look of a dog
can attract strangers to it like a magnet. These are people who
wish to possess it without knowing what it can actually do in
the field of work. Beauty is said to be in the eye of the beholder,
but people's opinions and ideas of what is aesthetically pleasing
are as varied as the colours of fallen autumn leaves.

'You're after the wrong one,' I replied truthfully. 'The little
black one is the better dog.' A smile struggled to break though
on his wrinkled face.

'I know which one of them I want.'

His choice was dictated solely by what the dog looked like,
and I was reminded of a fable about the snipe.

A female snipe met a hunter and implored him not to shoot
any of her chicks. On asking how he would recognise them,
she told him he could not make a mistake as they were the
most handsome birds he would ever meet. Later that day, the
ugliest looking bird the hunter had ever seen got up out of the
deep, russet bracken and the sportsman's shots rang out. But it
was one of the female snipe's young that he had killed, for the

159

hunter's idea of beauty was one thing and the mother snipe's was another. Just like the snipe, a lot of lurcher buffs view dogs in this way.

The dog for which this man pestered me so much was a 27-inch, rough-haired, wheaten-coloured dog called Fly. His looks much resembled those of a younger version of my good friend, Perry Fairfax's, dog, Fluke, and also of Flame, and a lurcher of another acquaintance of mine, the late Basil Smalley. All these dogs were highlighted in Ted Walsh's excellent book, *Lurchers and Longdogs*. Although Fly wasn't bred from these excellent dogs, he did come from similar deerhound ancestry, so to be fair on the gypsy, his choice wasn't a dud.

Both Fairfax and Smalley owned excellent farms in north Northumberland, with plentiful supplies of hares on which I have been invited to work my dogs many times. Whenever I have coursed on these areas, Fly matched the achievements of various dogs, both living and gone, belonging to these eminent landowners. He would, however, have to take second

Bes and Fly with a morning's bag

place in the presence of the dog the tinker discounted.

Over the decades I must have witnessed so many dogs that were kept only because of their looks, satisfying the quirks and fads of people who did most of their killing in their imaginations or as they propped up a bar in their local social club. I have also lost count of the number of dogs classed as ugly but which did all their owner's talking where it counts: out in the fields.

I have already mentioned the hunting virtues of Northumberland lurcherman, Ron Murray's, Assassin dog. During the late 70s, many lurcher enthusiasts from Ashington, Newbiggin-by-the-Sea and Lynemouth grouped together to form a match against hares with their dogs. The Assassin was paired against a lurcher called Fiver, a name bestowed upon the dog because that was what it cost to buy. On the day, it was Fiver that won the course, against a dog that was virtually unbeatable. Fiver was also the eventual winner of the competition. Now, I remember observing Fiver working, it was not a great looking lurcher, no super model, just a lurcher that always gave 100 percent.

Another example that sticks in my mind with crystal clarity was when Billy Mercel and I visited acquaintances on a gypsy camp near Bedlington in Northumberland during the late 80s. Our dogs, Bes and Paddy, were prepped and ready for action and, although they were primarily lampers, they had accounted for over 200 hares between them. The morning's sport was to take place on small fields that circumnavigated the campsite.

When ready, our traveller hosts brought forth the ugliest dog I have ever seen. Not only was he unsightly, he was a virtual cripple, with toes missing from three of his four feet. Boy, as the dog was called, had a bulky, straight front that caused him to resemble a hyena. He was also short coupled and poorly angulated, a dog that, if in the show ring, would have been thrown out with the rubbish

There was dead silence, then our heads shook mockingly and sniggers quickly developed into full-blown shouts of laughter. 'What do you think you're going to do with him?' I asked. The man just smiled as he stooped, took a piece of orange baling twine from the confines of his jacket pocket and wrapped it around the old dog's neck.

'Come on then Boy, time for a run,' he whispered. As if he had chanted some form of Romany incantation, the dog rose. Billy and I looked at each other, turned, and we all set off eager for the feel of the brittle stubble beneath our feet. Needless to say we were proved wrong in our judgments of Boy. Our lurchers may have produced all the goods and done all the running, but it was old Mason's dog that took the only hare on the day.

Good-looking lurchers come from various sources, but deerhound crosses are notoriously handsome animals, lurcher-show judges' dreams. In the show ring, where beauty takes precedence over working ability, these dogs always catch the attention of the well-trained eyes of an experienced evaluator. This is an area where looks count, indeed, probably one of the only situations where looks count.

'Well, are you parting with him? Name yer price.' The traveller at the horse-driving trials took a wad of money from his pocket as thick as a scaffold-pipe.

I have been around them long enough to know the ways of travellers: turn your head and they think they have you on the run, dither and you are half way to defeat. I looked him straight in the eyes, with neither a frown nor a smile.

'Look, the dog's not for sale.' He switched his attention to my little black un and I read what was coming next.

'Don't even think about it.'

AUTHOR'S NOTE

I hope that this book will be of some assistance to those who read it. I did not write it with the expectation or wish that everyone should rush out and buy a deerhound or a composite bred from them. Its aim is to highlight the working abilities of these dogs, entirely through my experience with them.

To better illustrate the potential talents of these dogs, I have added two separate anthologies of short, true hunting stories to complement the factual descriptions. I believe this adds a new dimension to the book which I hope, as a result, will entertain as well as educate. Several of these accounts are based on articles of mine that were published in various magazines in the English sporting press from the mid-90s onwards.

I have deliberately given a brief insight into all of the quarry species these dogs can be used to hunt, for I believe firmly that in order to become a more successful hunter we should know as much as possible about the prey we so diligently seek.

I have discussed various forms of hunting: day-light work on rabbits, organised hare coursing, ferreting and lamping. I have written candidly about all of them and about how my dogs have fared at them all. I have made many comparisons, which I hope will assist the reader to make up his or her mind as to just how good, or not so good, these dogs can be.

Last but not least, I have mentioned some of the people

with whom I have had the privilege to hunt: characters all, as lurcherdom is full of such people. We all know them or someone like them, and I have highlighted those known to me and who, I believe, will be of interest to readers.

Working Deerhounds, Lurchers and Longdogs is an important book. It chronicles much of what took place when such hunting with dogs was legal, before the advent of the 2004 Hunting Act. It will be a reference for the future, for those who will never experience the thrill of hunting with dogs or understand what went on in the fields when nature was protected for sport and consequently the British countryside was the envy of Europe.

I am a firm advocate of the saying, 'What goes around comes around.' I have been lucky to have lived and hunted in an era when deerhound-blooded lurchers and longdogs were unsurpassed. I have also witnessed the rise and subsequent fall in various designer crosses and now, in 2006, a revival in interest in working deerhounds and deerhound composites.

I do, however, feel that we will never again see the same quality of working deerhounds. The Hunting Act was the last nail in their coffin. So many of the traits and virtues that were bywords for the quality of the breed will now be buried and unused, because the dogs are no longer worked in appropriate circumstances. And the knock-on effect will have far reaching consequences for their hybrids.

Bill Doherty

Ashington
October 2006